D1611461

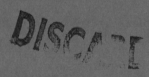

DISCARD

# MEMORIES OF THOMAS WOLFE

## A PICTORIAL COMPANION TO *LOOK HOMEWARD, ANGEL*

# MEMORIES OF

# THOMAS WOLFE

## A PICTORIAL COMPANION TO *LOOK HOMEWARD, ANGEL*

BY

JOHN CHANDLER GRIFFIN

SUMMERHOUSE PRESS
*Columbia, South Carolina*

**Published in Columbia, South Carolina
by the Summerhouse Press**

Copyright © 1996 by Summerhouse Press

ISBN #1-887714-08-1 (hardcover)

Manufactured in the United States of America.

First Edition

Photographs are reproduced here by permission of
Paul Gitlin, Adminstrator, C.T.A.,
The Estate of Thomas Wolfe

Additional Photo Credits:
Pack Memorial Public Library, Asheville, N.C.
19, 25, 26, 33, 34, 35, 36, 38, 39, 40, 42, 44, 46, 48, 50, 52, 55, 56, 57, 61, 62, 64, 67, 68,
69, 70, 71, 73, 74, 75, 76, 78, 81, 83, 84, 88, 92, 94, 95, 98, 100, 101, 103, 105, 110

University of North Carolina Library, Chapel Hill, N.C.
Pages  3, 27, 29, 31, 32, 35, 37, 41, 42, 43, 47, 51, 53, 55, 66, 68, 83, 91, 99, 104, 107, 116

**Library of Congress Cataloging-in-Publication Data**

Griffin, John  Chandler, 1936-
    Memories of Thomas Wolfe : a pictorial companion to "Look
homeward,  angel" / by John  Chandler Griffin.
        p.  cm.
        Includes  bibliographical  references.
        ISBN 1-887714-08-1
        1. Wolfe, Thomas, 1900-1938.  Look homeward, angel.  2.  Novelists,
American--20th century--Family relationships.  3.  Novelists,
American--20th century--Biography.  4.  Wolfe, Thomas, 1900-1938-
-Friends and associates.  5.  Wolfe, Thomas, 1900-1938--Homes and
haunts.  6. Literary landmarks--South Carolina.  7.  Literary
landmarks--North Carolina.  8.  Wolfe, Thomas, 1900-1938--Family.
I.  Title.
PS3545.0337L683   1996
813'.52--dc20
[B]                                                 96-30602
                                                      CIP

# CONTENTS

INTRODUCTION: THE STORY OF A BOOK     7

I. LOOK HOMEWARD, BROTHER: FRED WOLFE REMEMBERS     13

II. THE INCREDIBLE JOURNEY 1851-1899
    WILLIAM OLIVER WOLFE: FROM YORK SPRINGS TO ASHEVILLE     25
    W.O. MARRIES JULIA WESTALL     34
    THOMAS WOLFE'S SIBLINGS ARE BORN     40

III. THE YEARLY YEARS 1900-1912
    TOM'S BIRTH     43
    THE TRIP TO ST. LOUIS AND GROVER'S DEATH     45
    JULIA PURCHASES THE OLD KENTUCKY HOME     51
    TOM ENTERS THE ORANGE STREET SCHOOL     54
    EFFIE MARRIES ED GAMBRELL     57
    BEN BECOMES A PAPER BOY     61
    MABEL BECOMES AN ENTERTAINER     65

IV. THE NORTH STATE YEARS 1912-1916
    THE NORTH STATE FITTING SCHOOL AND MARGARET ROBERTS     73
    FRED ENTERS GEORGIA TECH AND DRIVES W.O.'S CAR     78
    THE ANGEL     82
    MABLE MARRIES RALPH WHEATON     84

V. THE COLLEGE YEARS 1916-1920
    TOM ENTERS THE UNIVERSITY OF NORTH CAROLINA     91
    TOM MEETS CLARA PAUL     94
    BEN'S DEATH     106
    TOM BECOMES A SUCCESSFUL PLAYWRIGHT     109
    TOM'S GRADUATION     113

CHRONOLOGY OF EVENTS IN THE LIFE OF THOMAS WOLFE     115

SELECTED BIBLIOGRAPHY     118

*As Always*

**To Betty and Alexis**

# Introduction
# The Story of a Book

*"...our lives are haunted by a Georgia slattern,*
*because a London cutpurse went unhung."*—*from* LHA

Dear Reader:

This book truly had its genesis back in the Spring of 1965, my freshman year at Armstrong State College in Savannah, Georgia, where I was majoring in Anthropology, driving a '58 Olds Rocket 88, wearing pegged pants and sporting a heavily waxed flattop. That was back when I had this fixed idea that I hated Thomas Wolfe. In fact, I'd hated him for a good while, ever since my high school English teacher, Mrs. Doris Parker Johnson, had assigned our class to read "Only the Dead Know Brooklyn."

That was back in McColl, a tiny hamlet nestled in the swamps of coastal South Carolina, where the value of everything from cars to doughnuts was measured in how many pounds of cotton it'd take to pay for it. My fellow students and I were all the sons and daughters of storekeepers, small farmers and cotton mill workers—kids who rarely visited the Metropolitan Museum of Art. But now Mrs. Johnson had assigned us to read "Only the Dead Know Brooklyn."

I still remember how it went. It was a cold, gray morning in April, with dark storm clouds hanging low. In the classroom that morning, Mrs. Johnson opened her anthology, then very sweetly asked me to explain to the class just what the story was all about.

"Well, I really didn't get too much out of it," I said apologetically, "but it seemed to be about a bunch of Yankees who talked funny. I'm not really sure about that." I looked around at my fellow classmates for confirmation that this story was totally beyond human analysis. Their anxious silence seemed to settle the matter. Nobody had gotten very much out of it.

At any rate, that was my somewhat grim introduction to Thomas Wolfe, and for some time after that I'd told everyone who would listen that Thomas Wolfe was probably the worst writer in history. Not as bad as Henry James or William Dean Howells, maybe, but certainly right up there among those boring wretches—or wretched bores. I didn't even like his name—Wolfe. It seemed somehow to conjure up all sorts of hostile and threatening images.

Ah, but now, as the reader already suspects, the story takes a sudden (and predictable) twist. I was speaking with a fellow student at college, one Bill Martin, now an English professor at Armstrong, who informed me just before class one morning that Thomas Wolfe was the finest author in the history of American literature. (And perhaps I should point out here that Bill Martin remains the only person I've ever heard use the word "phthisic" in everyday conversation.)

But I told Bill that I hated Thomas Wolfe and everything he'd ever written.

---

*The discerning reader will note that any similarities between this little ditty and Thomas Wolfe's* The Story of a Novel *are purely coincidental.*

"You hate *Look Homeward, Angel?*"

Not only was Bill an ace student, he was also a champion weight lifter. So I didn't really want to press the point.

"Well, actually, I haven't read *Look Homeward, Angel.*"

"What have you read?"

"Only the Dead Know Brooklyn."

"Well, that story's really atypical of Wolfe. To tell the truth, I don't care too much for it myself. But let me urge you to read *Look Homeward, Angel.*"

"I wouldn't read it for a million dollars."

"I'll make you a deal." He reverently handed me his own copy of the novel. "Read it, and if you don't like it, I'll give you ten dollars."

"You've got a deal." Already I was making big plans for spending that ten bucks.

To make a long story short, I took the novel home, began reading it, and found to my surprise that I couldn't put it down.

And after all these years I still regard it as the most personal book I've ever read, filled with characters and events that I've known and experienced all my life. Truly, even today I can identify with every personage in that book. At times, I'm Eugene; at other times I'm Ben, or maybe Fred, or Frank, or even old W.O. himself. I can recall at various times in my life feeling the same driving impulses that motivate these characters, and I've at least considered pursuing courses of action similar to the ones they chose. As for *Angel's* Southern setting, I have always felt right at home in Altamont.

In a word, I've always known, deep down in the inner-most places of my heart, that I am somehow a member of that wild Gant clan, as much as Eugene himself.

But let us skip ahead a decade (try to picture leaves peeling away from the calendar, the way it's done in the movies.) By 1974, I held a Ph.D. in American Literature and had been teaching at USC-Lancaster for several years. Also, being young and foolish, I had attempted to teach *Look*

*Homeward, Angel* to my American Lit classes every semester. As a part of that course I would load up our school bus and take the students on a tour of Asheville. We all considered it a special treat to stop off in Spartanburg for a brief visit with Fred Wolfe.

Fred ("good old big-hearted Luke") lonely now after the recent death of his wife of many years, was always most cordial to us and played the perfect host. And, true to form, he inevitably became the darling of every coed who met him.

Then it was on to Asheville and the Old Kentucky Home, where Myra Champion, a dear lady (now deceased), would meet us and show us around town, taking us to Pack Square, Riverside Cemetery, and other points of interest.

In 1975, I invited Fred to USC-Lancaster where he regaled a packed audience on a warm August evening with his memories of Tom. Among those in attendance that night was Dr. John Fulenwider, a Pageland physician and a noted collector of Thomas Wolfe memorabilia. John and Fred had been friends for years, and John had dinner with us following Fred's presentation.

He informed me that he had donated all his Wolfe materials to St. Mary's College in Raleigh, where his daughter was enrolled as a student. He also pointed out that St. Mary's was hosting a Wolfe Fest in October and asked if I would like to be on the program.

"Well, gee, I don't know," I replied honestly. "I really don't know anything about Wolfe. I think *Look Homeward, Angel* is a fine work, but I certainly don't consider myself a Wolfe scholar by any stretch of the imagination."

"Well, if you come up with anything in the next couple of weeks just let me know. We'll slap you right on the program."

The next day it occurred to me that Fred had stated on several occasions that Tom had made a special trip home just to get the old family photo album when writing *Look Homeward, Angel.* He wanted to look at the old photos in hopes of jogging his memory, Tom had said. Then it also occurred to me that comparing the old Wolfe family photos with passages from *Angel* might prove a worthwhile project.

To that end, I visited Pack Memorial Library in Asheville and the Thomas Wolfe Collection at the University of North Carolina to research photos that I thought would be appropriate to such a project. I also visited with Wolfe's nephews (Effie's sons) in Anderson and Greenville, who made their personal collections available to me. In the end, I collected some five hundred photos of Wolfe, his kindred and friends. Of those, there were about one hundred and fifty photos that could well illustrate *Look Homeward, Angel*.

I did make a presentation at St. Mary's College, and it was well received, enough that I decided to go public with it, or take it downtown, so to speak. Over the next few years, I made presentations at several more Wolfe fests, as well as at the annual meeting of the Southern Philological Association at Winthrop University, the Southern Cultural Society Meeting, at the University of South Carolina, the Southern Renascence Conference at the University of Southern Maine, and at the Old Kentucky Home on the occasion of Wolfe's birthday in 1980.

Already I was thinking that publishing a pictorial companion to *Look Homeward, Angel* would be an excellent idea.

It was about then that, for certain financial reasons with which many college professors can identify, I became sidetracked. Instead of pursuing my work on Wolfe, I would become a freelance writer. I would become a sports historian, for which there seemed to be a bustling market, and I would become filthy rich.

And so for the next fifteen years that's pretty much how my life went, hacking out a weekly sports feature for several major newspapers, as well as occasional articles for various magazines and several sports books.

But through it all, Thomas Wolfe was never far from my thoughts. Such being the case, in January of 1996 with retirement staring me in the face, I decided to get cranking with my long-delayed Thomas Wolfe book. So I selected certain Wolfe photos that would illustrate *Look Homeward, Angel*, stacked them on my desk, arranged them in chronological order, flipped on the PageMaker on my computer and began to write.

Less than two months later I had compiled the humble little book that you are, at this very moment, holding.

So now, thank God, for the first time in many years my conscience is clear.

And that's the story of how this book, whatever its value to Thomas Wolfe scholarship may be, came finally into being. Truly, it has been germinating for the past twenty years.

But even at that, I enjoyed the advantage of having so much help along the way. And I needed it. For over the years some of my facts had become confused with other facts, and even confused with other fictions. And would doubtlessly have remained confused had it not been for the very generous criticisms and advice offered me by such peerless Wolfe scholars as Joseph Flora, Aldo Magi, Ted Mitchell, John Idol, and Alice Cotten. To them I am most grateful. Without the help of the staffs at Pack Memorial Public Library in Asheville, and at the University of North Carolina, this book would not have been possible.

Also I wish to express my thanks to the Thomas Wolfe Society for the tireless support and encouragement that august body has offered me.

My thanks, too, to Paul Gitlin and the Thomas Wolfe Estate for permission to publish this.

As for you, Dear Reader, especially if you're a beginning Wolfe scholar (for whom this work is mostly intended), I sincerely hope you will enjoy this book, and I trust you will "get something out of it."

*—Your Pal,*
*Good old Bruce-John Griffin*
*June, 1996*

# MEMORIES OF THOMAS WOLFE

## A PICTORIAL COMPANION TO *LOOK HOMEWARD, ANGEL*

A SHOT OF FRED AND TOM TAKEN DURING A VISIT WITH EFFIE AT HER HOME ON LAUREL STREET IN ANDERSON, S.C., IN 1937. IT SHOULD BE NOTED THAT FRED STOOD 6'3", WHICH SHOULD GIVE THE READER A GOOD IDEA OF TOM'S GIANT DIMENSIONS.

# I

## LOOK HOMEWARD, BROTHER
## FRED WOLFE REMEMBERS

*As soon as Tom returned to America he came home to get the old family photo album.  He said he needed it to help jog his memory of things that had happened when he was growing up.  Some of the photos in that album are described perfectly in* **Angel***.*
                                                                          *——Fred Wolfe*

Few who have read *Look Homeward, Angel,* Thomas Wolfe's haunting masterpiece of fictional autobiography, can ever forget Luke Gant, the elder brother of Eugene and a living, breathing, three-dimensional creature of flesh and blood if ever an author created one.  A veritable chameleon of impulses, it is Luke the practical who recruits and captains a small army of school urchins (including Eugene) to go out on the streets of Asheville and hawk the *Saturday Evening Post;* and it is he, Luke the resourceful, who uses threats and cajolery to rally the spirits of that same little ragtag army when sales are slow and the boys yearn to throw down their burdens and fly to the friendly hearths of home.  In later years it's Luke the compassionate who comforts the lovelorn Eugene after his ill-fated journey to Norfolk in search of his lost sweetheart.  And it is Luke the avenger whose terrible wrath devastates those myopic policemen who had the audacity to interrupt the erring Eugene's drinking spree through the streets of Spartanburg and toss him in the city clink, breaking his nose in the process.

According to Thomas Wolfe, Luke was a lifelong stutterer, a speech impediment that became more pronounced during moments of intense excitement.  Wolfe recalls, for example,  the family sitting in the living room of their home one warm spring evening, while Luke,  a high school senior at the time, busied himself courting a somewhat busty young lady on the front porch.  During a sudden lull in the family conversation, says Wolfe, the unmistakeable strains of Luke's voice came wafting romantically through the open window: "Can I lay my head on your b-b-b-breast?"

For the rest of the evening, says Wolfe, the house shook with silent laughter.

Sometimes funny, sometimes tragic, always loveable, Luke Gant truly had as his destiny to provide that perfect dash of madness to a family already endowed with more than its share of eccentricity.

Here now to share his recollections of that family is Luke Gant, or Fred Wolfe as he was known in real life, telling the story in his own words—minus the "whah-whah-whahs."

---

*The following article is based on a series of taped interviews the author conducted with Fred Wolfe at his home in Spartanburg, S.C., in 1974-75.  Copies of these tapes were later donated to the Thomas Wolfe Collection at St. Mary's College in Raleigh, N.C.*

*It should also be noted that some Wolfe scholars have expressed skepticism concerning a few of Fred's recollections (Tom's relationship with Aline Bernstein, for example, his religious views and so on).*

THE WOLFE FAMILY, ON THE EVENING OF TOM'S FUNERAL IN 1938, GRIEVES IN THE
LIVING ROOM OF THE OLD KENTUCKY HOME IN ASHEVILLE. (L-R:) FRANK, JULIA,
EFFIE, MABEL AND FRED.

## Fred Wolfe Remembers:

I think it was Tom's feeling for people that makes *Look Homeward, Angel* as popular today as ever, and maybe more so. You see, each succeeding generation is told by the previous one about *Angel* and they see that, since we are all related emotionally and mentally, it reminds them of themselves, of things they have done and been involved in. They see in Eugene Gant a picture of themselves as youngsters. I think that's the reason for Tom's continued popularity, not only with *Angel* but with his other novels as well. But regardless of how fine *Angel* and *Of Time and the River* may be, and I think highly of them, though I don't care too much for *The Web and the Rock*, I still think that *You Can't Go Home Again* is the finest thing Tom ever wrote.

As for my family, my father was William Oliver Wolfe, born in 1851. He was Pennsylvania Dutch, born up around Gettysburg near York Springs.

Papa had very little schooling, so when he grew up he moved down to Baltimore and served an apprenticeship to a stone engraver. Four years later he came on down to Columbia where he put the caps on the State House. You know those eight columns on the porch of the State House? Well, Papa carved the caps that are on top of those columns. Then a year later he went up to Raleigh and did the same thing for the state insane asylum, and also the North Carolina State House.

Well, he settled in Raleigh and married twice there. His first wife was a woman by the name of Hattie Watson, daughter of a photographer. He divorced Hattie, and after waiting a year married a woman nine years older than he who was named Cynthia Hill. Later he brought Cynthia to Asheville for her health. She died but Papa stayed on and went into business there.

Now my mother, Julia Westall Wolfe, was a fine woman. She was not avaricious, as some critics have claimed. She did have a keen love for the ownership of property, but she came up the hard way in the very poor mountain family of Thomas Casey Westall. There

were eleven children in that family and they had to scratch for a living. But she did receive an education, such as it was, and she attended college in Hendersonville, enough so that she could teach school. But my mother's motive in accumulating property was to build up an estate that she could leave to her children.

And Tom was literally her eyeballs. When she went to Florida, or wherever, she always took him with her. Tom owed an awful lot to Mama.

People have asked me how Tom chose the name Gant for the Wolfe family in *Look Homeward, Angel*. That came about in sort of a strange way. When Tom was a boy, he and Papa would sometimes spend the weekends with our older married sister Effie Wolfe Gambrell down in Anderson, S.C. Papa and Tom would take the train as far as Greenville, then they'd take a trolley car that ran to Belton and Anderson. It was called the Piedmont Northern Railway and has long been out of service. Well, there was a little way station between Greenville and Belton and the name of it was Gantt. The trolley would stop there and everyone would get off for a while and partake of refreshments, have a picnic, and the boys would play baseball. Tom said he always remembered Gantt as a wonderful place, and later decided to give us the name Gant in his first book.

As most people know, I play the role of Luke in *Angel*. I guess Tom made me out to be a little more bizarre than I am in that book, though I am bizarre enough, God knows.

And in Tom's first book of short stories, *From Death Till Morning*, he has a story about him and me called "Circus At Dawn." It's all about how we'd go down in the dark of the morning and cross the tracks at the Asheville railway station where they had this string of circus cars. You see, that was back in the days of the big circus and they would give a big parade before the performance. But all that passed many years ago. The excitement of the circus has ended.

One of the saddest episodes in *Angel* concerns our

Following Tom's funeral on September 18, 1938, grieving family members gather by his grave at Riverside Cemetery in Asheville. (L-R:) Frank, Julia, Mary (Fred's wife), and Fred. (This photo was snapped by Tom's sister Mabel Wolfe Wheaton.)

Following Tom's death, Maxwell Perkins, Tom's editor at Scribners, assisted Fred in settling Tom's somewhat muddled financial affairs. Here, Fred and Perkins take in the sights of New York.

older brother Grover and his death in St. Louis in 1904 when I was ten years old. I remember the night Grover died. It broke my mother's heart. We'd been out to St. Louis for the World's Fair and Mama opened a boardinghouse there. It was on Academy Street and she paid $250 a month for the lease.

The fair was over in October. Grover took sick with typhoid fever and it turned into pneumonia and it killed him. He was only twelve years old. You see, Grover and Ben, they were the twins, were twelve years old. Grover was a brunette and vivacious and saw the bright side of the world. But Ben was just the opposite. He was blond and all scowl and very gray.

Tom was only four at the time, but he swore that he remembered it all. He heard a great deal about it from Mama, but he did have a retentive memory. I guess Tom was sort of a combination of Ben and Grover. He was always obsessed with a sense of loneliness, but that was only when he was by himself. Put him in a crowd, big or small, and he would scintillate like a star. He loved to tell jokes and be the life of the party.

Another sad scene in *Angel* concerns Ben's death in 1918. And Tom's description of that occasion, by the way, is very accurate. We did, Tom and I, go down to the diner in the early morning hours and eat and speak with the undertaker. It happened just that way. And we also picked out Ben's casket, and the undertaker, whom Tom calls Horse Hines, said, "Now don't you think he looks fine? Don't you think I've done a good job?" And Tom began to laugh wildly. That has been a scene of amusement to all who've read *Angel*, and it's all factual.

I've heard people express bewilderment about the scene in *Angel* where Tom meets Ben's ghost. But I explain it this way: Tom is remembering the day he came home from school, from UNC. He crosses Pack Square in the cold of early morning, and he sees a familiar figure with his foot upon the iron rail of Papa's marble shop. And Tom comes up and says, "My God, Ben, that can't be you. I saw them bury you two years ago." And Ben says, "Who else, you little fool? Why of course it's me." Now Tom was doing what? He was

reciting a vision. That scene never really happened, but it makes good reading.

And Tom does the same thing with the death of Papa. Do you remember the little golden haired boy? He is walking ahead of Papa down the lane and Papa is following. But Papa can never catch up with him. My father is lying in bed in the back room of the house dying and this is the vision he has. He is the old man who cannot catch up with the golden haired boy. Then he wakes up. He is near death, and he says, "Julia, I've seen them all." And he mentions his family back in Pennsylvania, all long dead and gone, and he tells of his vision of the little golden haired boy. But this scene was pure fiction.

Yes, it's true, Tom did always feel a great deal of affection for Ben, and I can tell you the reason. You see, there was a close affinity between Tom and Ben. They seemed to have been set apart from the rest of us. In other words, they were in tune with one another. And Ben, who only went through the tenth grade, always defended Tom and urged him to go to college. Tom would say, "Ben, why didn't you go to college?" And Ben would say, "Well, it's too late. They wouldn't send me. They'll tell you they're broke but don't you let them do it. You get every damned cent out of them you can and you go to college. Papa has the money to send you." And of course he had. Mama sent Tom to the North State Fitting School there in Asheville, the same as high school. And when he finished there he matriculated at UNC. He lacked six weeks of being sixteen at the time. That was in 1916.

The first six months that Tom was there he had a pretty rough time because he'd never been away from home before and his clothes didn't fit—his pants were halfway up to his knees and his sleeves came up above his wrists. Later he dressed better than that. But there were a lot of boys from Asheville down there and they liked Tom, and what they did, they ribbed him. But Tom was sensitive and he almost didn't go back after Christmas. But he did go back, and he didn't have to find those boys, they found him. They'd seen what he

SIXTY-ONE YEARS OLD IN 1955, THE STILL HANDSOME FRED WAS ALWAYS EAGER FOR ANY OPPORTUNITY TO CHAMPION TOM'S CAUSE.

could do, what talent he had. He was, at one time or another, editor of *The Daily Tarheel* and *The Tar Baby,* their newspaper and literary magazine.

Then he enlisted in The Carolina Playmakers. They wrote and performed one-act folk plays. Tom wrote four or five of those. His most successful one was *The Return of Buck Gavin,* which he wrote in 1919, all about a mountaineer moonshiner. Well, they performed that one for twenty-five years up at UNC.

When he finished at UNC in 1920 he talked Mama into sending him to Harvard to get his master's degree. Now anybody knows you can get a master's in one year.

But Tom was using that degree business only as an excuse. What he really wanted was to study under Dr. George Pierce Baker who conducted the 47 Workshop in the School of Drama at Harvard, writing three-act plays. Eugene O'Neill went through the 47 Workshop. But Tom's plays were entirely too long. They were long and drawn out, like an accordian that you can't bring back in. Such were his plays. He couldn't condense them.

So the Theater Guild in New York offered to produce *Welcome to Our City* and *Manorhouse* if Tom would delete some scenes. Well, he tried. He would go off for a few months and write, but when he came back, instead of deleting and condensing scenes, he would have added two or three more scenes and introduced a half dozen new characters. So he didn't know what to do. He became what is commonly known as a frustrated playwright. That's when he started teaching at NYU.

Then he made his first trip to Europe, and it was there that he finally found himself and his proper channel of writing, and that's when he began making notes for his first novel, *Look Homeward, Angel.*

As soon as Tom returned to America he came home to get the old family photo album. He said he needed it to help jog his memory of things that had happened when he was growing up. Some of the photos in that album are described perfectly in *Angel.*

Of course the *Angel* manuscript was long and drawn out, too. Max Perkins was Tom's editor at Scribners, and there were times when Tom felt that Max was cutting out chunks of his heart.

Still, Tom had to get his manuscript into publishable form. The original manuscript of *Angel* was almost one million words long but when he and Max were finished with it, cutting it down and changing its title, it made a novel of about five hundred and fifty-six pages. Max had a lot of trouble with Tom. Tom was temperamental and did not want a word left out of

AN AGED FRED HOLDS A FIRST EDITION OF *LOOK HOMEWARD, ANGEL* THAT TOM PRESENTED TO HIM IN 1929.

anything he ever wrote. In fact, anything that was left out of *Angel* would reappear later in Tom's other three novels. He never lost a thing.

You'll note that Tom dedicated *Angel* to his dear friend Aline Bernstein ("To A. B."), and he also gave her the seventeen handwritten ledgers that was the original manuscript of *Angel*. Of course today they're invaluable. But Aline accepted them. For Tom that was like giving away his life's blood. Well, Aline kept the manuscript for a few years, then following the Spanish Civil War, when so many refugees needed help, when they were having those auction sales in New York to raise money, she auctioned it off for two million dollars. The buyer donated it to Harvard University and it became part of the William B. Wisdom Collection. That's where it is now.

In 1936 Tom went to Germany. He didn't care much for the English or the French, but the Germans were the first Europeans to publish him. Plus Papa's people were from Germany and so Tom was eager to go and visit the land of his ancestors.

They were having the Olympic games in Berlin and Tom's German publishers invited him to be their guest in their box for the games. Their box, by the way, flanked Hitler's box. That was the year that Jessie Owens, the great Negro athlete, won four gold medals, and every time they'd bring him out there to crown him, Tom would jump to his feet and give a rousing western North Carolina war-whoop and yell, "Come on, Jessie, you're doing this for America!" And Tom said each time he did that Hitler and Goering would turn around and give him a baleful stare. But it didn't bother Tom one bit.

The real reason that Tom went to Germany was because his publishers there owed him 50,000 Reichmarks, but they said he'd have to come to Germany to get them and that he'd have to spend them there. He could only take fifty marks out of the country. So he went to Berlin and they paid him and he stayed there for three months, or until he'd spent all the money.

You see, the Germans would search your baggage at the border and if you were caught with more than fifty marks, why they'd pull you off the train and arrest you.

Well, Tom met a Jewish boy on the train coming out and he wrote an article about him called "I Have A Thing To Tell You" in *The New Republic*. This young Jew was scared to death. He had a visa and he was leaving the country, but at the checkpoint the Germans caught him. Just before the police came aboard, the Jew handed Tom 500 marks and said, "Take it. You've already been examined." So Tom did. The Germans

Fred and his beloved wife of many years, the former Mary Burriss of Anderson, S.C. (It should be noted that of all Tom's siblings, only Frank and Effie would ever have children.)

opened the boy's suitcase and found several thousand marks in it and they pulled him off the train. That was the last Tom ever saw of that boy. He said they doubtlessly threw him in a concentration camp and in all probability killed him.

But Tom really made very little from his writings. During the late-1930s he was the guest speaker at the Literary Awards Dinner in New York, and he said, "I've written four novels and several works of short stories. But other than my little income from the short stories, I doubt if my whole revenue would total more than fifty thousand dollars." It was truly ironic. You see, Tom died and left a will and I read his will the year before he died. He had left my mother ten thousand dollars. And that was about it, except for the interest left to the other heirs in his estate. I said, "Well, Tom, have you got ten thousand dollars to leave Mama?" And he said, "Fred, I've got a literary estate that will probably be worth the money." But at that time he was essentially broke.

It was soon after our conversation that Tom decided to change publishers. He went from Scribner's to Harpers because he was so sensitive to criticism. Bernard DeVoto and several other detractors began worrying Tom to death and he didn't work for a whole year because of them. Max Perkins said, "Tom, they're insane and they're foolish and everybody knows it. I've been your editor but the reality is all yours. So go back to work and write the truth." But Tom wouldn't listen. He only said, "I want to change publishers."

Cass Canfield of Harpers met Tom at the old Chelsea Hotel in New York and he said, "Tom, we will take anything you write and publish it. And we want to do one more thing for you. We understand you've had your royalties dribbled out to you five hundred dollars at a time. So, if you'll come with Harpers, we'll give you an advance check for ten thousand dollars." So Tom went with Harpers and they gave him that check for ten thousand dollars.

That was in 1937, the year before Tom died. During the next year he wrote furiously. He said to me, "Fred, everything in the past is dead. That's the way I feel since leaving Scribner's. I've changed publishers and become a harlot. I want to go back to Scribner's."

But of course he didn't. He accepted the Harpers check for ten thousand dollars and deposited it in the Chase National Bank. But for the rest of his life he lived off the money he made from his short stories. Later, when we were in Seattle and Tom was dying, he told me that the Harpers money was still in the bank. He said, "If anything happens to me, Fred, call Mr. Hattiwall, president of Chase, and he'll tell you about my affairs." Of course when Tom died at Johns Hopkins in September, I had the money transferred to his estate.

Now it bothers me that some of the critics have called Tom's religious views into question. He was not a great church goer, it is true, but whenever he was in Asheville he would always call on Dr. N. F. Caudle, pastor of the First Presbyterian Church where we all grew up. Why Tom knew more about the Bible than the average preacher. It has been said that he was an atheist, but that is a lie, a damned lie. He was anything but an atheist. He believed in a hereafter and he often so expressed himself. When he writes "I shall leave this land for a greater land more kind than home" he is not expressing atheism. He is referring to the hereafter. Later, when he lay on his deathbed, he wrote to Max Perkins, "If I come through this, Max, if I come through this, in some strange way that I can't explain, I know before God that I will be a better man than I've ever been." No, Tom was anything but an atheist. He had liberal views, there's no question about it, but none that was tinted by atheism.

FRED ADDRESSES WOLFE DEVOTEES ON THE LAWN OF THE OLD KENTUCKY HOME IN 1975.

There's no question in my mind that Tom always knew he would die an early death. It was like a premonition. He said to me the year before he died, "Fred, do you think I'm going to die?" And I said, "Why, yes, Tom, we will all die. But what in the world has gotten into you?"

He said, "Well, I've worked so hard, and the doctor tells me I'm going to crash." Well, he should have taken a vacation right then. In his credo at the end of *You Can't Go Home Again* he writes, "And so Foxhall, old friend"—Foxhall being Max Perkins—"we have come to the end of the road that we were to go together. But before I go, I have just one more thing to tell you. Something has spoken to me in the night and told me that I shall die. I know not where. Saying: 'To lose the earth you know, for greater knowing; to lose the life you have, for greater life; to leave the friends you love, for greater loving; to find a land more kind than home, more large than earth—

'Whereon the pillars of this earth are founded, toward which the conscience of the world is tending. A wind is rising, and the rivers flow.'"

Unquestionably, Tom was predicting his own death. And in his last letter to Max Perkins—and I was with him when he wrote this letter, the last thing he ever wrote—he said, "Dear Max, old friend, I have been on a long journey, and I have seen the dark man very close, and I don't think I was too much afraid of him. But in some way that I can't explain, I hope to God that I am a better man. If I live, I will come back." Tom was almost insane with pain when he wrote that, and of course he died just a few days later.

Today I'm the only one left in the Wolfe family. But I was there and I saw it all, and what I've told you I've told from the heart. I'm very proud to be Tom Wolfe's brother, and I say that in all humility. I've tried to carry the torch as best I can. I only hope I haven't failed Tom or my family. I'm eighty-one now and I still carry on for them as best I can.

Thomas Wolfe devotees everywhere were saddened to learn of Fred's death in 1980. He is buried in Asheville's Riverside Cemetery surrounded by all those who were most dear to him in life.

# II

# THE INCREDIBLE JOURNEY
## (1863 - 1899)

*A destiny that leads the English to the Dutch is strange enough;
but one that leads from Epsom into Pennsylvania, and thence into
the hills that shut in Altamont over the proud coral cry of the cock,
and the soft stone smile of an angel, is touched by that dark miracle
of chance which makes new magic in a dusty world.*—*from* LHA

It was July 1, 1863, and the noonday heat was palpable as young William Oliver Wolf*, a boy of twelve, stood by the roadside gazing in awe at the long line of gray-clad Confederate veterans marching past on their way to Gettysburg.

The boy was tall for his age, slim of build, with flaxon blond hair and sharp, hawk-like features. An older relative, member of a Union cavalry brigade, had once remarked that Oliver had the cold, gray eyes of a sniper. It was an observation that a boy of twelve would remember with pride.

Behind him stood his home, a neat, two-story farmhouse, surrounded by forty acres of healthy green corn. The boy thoughtfully dug his bare toes into the sandy soil at the edge of the cornfield, then looked up startled as a bearded Confederate officer halted his horse before him.

The officer grinned and wiped his forehead with his tattered gray sleeve. "You got a name, Sonny?"

"Oliver," the boy stammered.

"Well, Oliver, it's mighty hot to be out here

fighting today. Do you think you could let me have a cold drink of water?"

"Yessir, I can do that!" Without another word, the boy whirled and ran to the stone well at the back of his house. He returned moments later carrying a bucket of water and a gourd dipper. The grateful officer drank deeply, then reached in his pocket and gave Oliver a dime for his troubles. "Now, son,

THE GRAVE STONE OF TOM'S GRANDFATHER, JACOB WOLF, A FARMER AND STONECUTTER, LOCATED IN GARDNER'S CEMETERY NEAR YORK SPRINGS, PENNSYLVANIA.

---

* Many years later, the boy became known as W.O. and added the "e" to "Wolf" after he married his second wife Cynthia and relocated to Asheville, N.C.

THE WOLF HOMEPLACE NEAR YORK SPRINGS.

there's a big fight going on just down the road," he warned. "Don't you go another step closer, not if you value your life."

"No, sir, I won't," the boy promised. Then he happily pocketed the dime, wiped the perspiration from his eyes and watched with admiration as the Southern officer rode away to meet his date with destiny.

In later years W.O. would remember that, despite the stifling heat and their obvious exhaustion, the Southern soldiers he observed that fateful day were in high spirits. He would recall that they were laughing and joking and that many were clowning around in black tophats, apparently lifted from some unfortunate shopkeeper in a nearby village.

A bearded young corporal, a member of Company F of the 14th North Carolina Infantry, flashing an eager grin, then approached W.O. He seated himself heavily on a rotted tree stump,

WILLIAM OLIVER WOLF AS A BOY OF SIXTEEN.

W. O. IN 1871.

carelessly dropped his musket at his feet, and helped himself to a long drink of water. Then he began fanning a swarm of gnats from his face with his battered gray hat.

"Say, Bub," he said, " do you know that man who you just give that drink of water to?"

W.O. shook his head. "I don't, but he was a mighty fine looking fellow."

"Why, that was General Fitzhugh Lee. Now you remember what he told you about staying away from that big fight down the road, and if you've got a dab of sense you'll save that dime he give you. It might be worth a lotta money some day."

And, sure enough, even in his later years, W.O. would relate the above story, then reach in his

W.O. IN 1876. NOW EMPLOYED IN RALEIGH, N.C., HE WAS A FASTIDIOUS DRESSER WHOSE QUICK YANKEE WIT MADE HIM A FAVORITE WITH ALL WHO KNEW HIM.

AT THE TOP OF THIS PHOTO, EXPRESSED IN HIS OWN EXAGGERATED, SELF-PITYING GANTIAN STYLE, HE HAS WRITTEN: *"Here I am before the smacks. How angelic and happy I look. Ah me."*

wallet and produce the dime given him by General Fitzhugh Lee during the great battle decades earlier.

Also, and incredible as it may seem, as a resident of Asheville, N.C., W.O. would again encounter that same corporal who had spoken with him so earnestly some twenty years earlier. His name was Bacchus Westall (jokingly called The Prophet). He was Julia Westall's uncle.

Born in 1851, W.O. was the seventh of nine children born to Jacob and Eleanor Heikes Wolf, descendants of the original German settlers who poured into Pennsylvania during the early 1700s. Like most of their neighbors, they were Quakers by persuasion, people who lived their religion on a daily basis. They farmed a small piece of land near York Springs, though many of their Wolf and Heikes kinsmen were professional stonecutters.

Following Jacob's death in 1860 Eleanor was left with nine children and very limited means of supporting them. Thus she did what many parents of the time did and farmed them out to other, more prosperous families in the region.

W.O. himself worked in a Union army livery stable, a situation that would last until war's end in 1865. At that time Eleanor (she would die in 1913 at the age of 96) appealed to him to pursue the occupation that had produced such a lively income for so many of his uncles and cousins. He should, and would, become a stonecutter.

W.O. had little formal education, but he was a young man of keen native intelligence and noted for his industry. Thus in 1866, accompanied by an older brother, Wesley (born in 1849), W.O. made his way by rail to Baltimore, and there the two boys were apprenticed to Hugh and Martin Sisson, owners of the oldest and most reputable marble shop in town. They took rooms at the nearby Farmers Hotel.

In 1869, having mastered his craft, he migrated to Columbia, S.C., where work was at last being completed on the State House, a huge edifice of the hardest granite. He was given a contract to carve the friezes atop the tall columns that ring the high front porch. It was laborious and painstaking work, but he was equal to the task and performed brilliantly (as any visitor to the South Carolina State House can see, even today).

Then in 1870 it was on to Raleigh, N.C., where he performed similar services at both the state insane asylum and the North Carolina State House.

Soon he had established a reputation as one of the most talented stonecutters in town, and in 1872 he entered into a partnership with John Cayton, and together they opened their own marble shop at the corner of Blount and Morgan Streets.

They hired a young apprentice, one John Watson, Jr., son of a local photographer. John's sister, Hattie Watson, was considered one of the most beautiful young ladies in Raleigh. W.O. met her and was immediately smitten.

Now a young man of twenty-one, the gangly 6'4" W.O. had lived a scarlet life for the past several years and was hardly reluctant to accept an occasional drink, a habit that tended to aggravate his already volatile temper. Indeed, his frequent companions during this period were the blades and harlots that frequented the barrooms of Raleigh, a social life that was in direct conflict with his strict Quaker upbringing. As a result, his evenings were times of wild revelry, his mornings times of black remorse.

In hopes of settling this conflict between good and evil that raged within his soul, he resolved to settle down to a sober and respectable life. Thus, after a brief courtship, in October of 1873 he married the dark-haired Hattie Watson. Respectability, at last, was within his grasp.

Still, everything considered, the Hattie–W.O. union hardly constituted a match made in heaven. Indeed, it was a marriage that would prove a total

THE BEAUTIFUL HATTIE WATSON, DAUGHTER OF A RALEIGH PHOTOGRAPHER BECAME W.O.'S FIRST WIFE IN 1873. SHE WAS GRANTED A DIVORCE IN 1876, CHARGING HER HUSBAND WITH "EXTREME CRUELTY" AND WITH BEING "PERMANENTLY AND INCURABLY IMPOTENT."

occurrence. They were sometimes visited by the Raleigh police who suggested that they should try to fight with a little more decorum.

By now Hattie had decided that the life of a pugilist was not what she had bargained for. And thus in 1876 she divorced her now totally humiliated husband, charging him with "extreme cruelty" (she claimed, for example, that on one occasion he beat her with a horsewhip) and with being "permanently and incurably impotent" (she cited no examples of his impotency, a matter of delicacy possibly). Their divorce proceedings became a celebrated affair and headlined in all the area newspapers.

Whereas a lesser man might have sworn off both liquor and women at this point, the doughty W.O. knocked down a pint of gin and swore that he'd find himself a wife who truly deserved a good man. Sure enough, within months he had met and courted a delightful redhaired spinster of impressive means named Cynthia Hill. She was thirty-six at the time of their marriage in October of 1879, some nine years older than W.O., and suffering from tuberculosis. Plus it was widely rumored that she had given birth to a child out of wedlock while on a "vacation trip" to New York.

As Fate would have it, W.O. and Cynthia decided to make their home in Asheville, some 250 miles to the west of Raleigh, where it was hoped that the dry mountain air would act as a balm for Cynthia's TB. (They also hoped to escape the social notoriety that had dogged their steps in recent years.)

Once arrived there, W.O. in June of 1880 opened a little marble shop on Pack Square and even built, with his own strong hands, a nice, rambling two-story house for Cynthia at 92 Woodfin Street.

Cynthia's maturity and quiet nature apparently neutralized W.O.'s insatiate desire for alcohol, and from all accounts, he rarely indulged now in the drinking sprees that had made him infa-

disaster for young W.O., socially as well as financially.

Despite his pious resolutions, he could not tolerate the sudden confinement and sobriety demanded by respectability and thus he revolted at the least opportunity—damn the torpedoes.

As the weeks lengthened into months his drinking sprees became more frequent and fights with the strong-willed Hattie an almost nightly

A shot taken of W.O. about 1873, the year of his marrige to Hattie Watson. Theirs was hardly a match made in heaven.

mous in Raleigh. After all, he was now a business-man, owned his own home, and had a respectable wife with a nice bank account. He was, he felt, a man to be envied and respected, a man of means.

He and Cynthia lived together very happily until her death in 1884. Then, once again, he found himself alone and desolate, "a stranger in a strange land."

Tom's mother, Julia Westall, was a descen-dant of several generations of solid Scotch-Irish people who had departed Pennsylvania to settle along the sparsely populated Appalachian Moun-tains from Maine to Georgia in the eighteenth century. Her father's people were apparently the scions of a Presbyterian minister who had settled near Asheville over a century earlier, while her

CYNTHIA HILL AT THE TIME OF HER MARRIAGE TO W.O. ODDLY ENOUGH, HER MATURE PERSONALITY (SHE WAS NINE YEARS OLDER THAN W.O.) SEEMS TO HAVE HAD A CALMING EFFECT ON HER RAMBUNCTIOUS HUSBAND, AND THEY LIVED TOGETHER VERY AMICABLY. W.O. BUILT THEIR HOME AT 92 WOODFIN STREET, AND HE INSISTED ON CARRYING THIS PICTURE OF HER IN HIS WALLET FOR THE REST OF HIS LIFE, LEADING HIS CHILDREN TO SNIGGERINGLY REFER TO HER AS "THE SAINTED CYNTHIA."

W.O. IN A PHOTO TAKEN SOON AFTER HE AND CYNTHIA HILL ARRIVED TO START A NEW LIFE IN ASHEVILLE FREE OF THEIR LURID PASTS.

*He was only past thirty, but he looked much older. His face was yellow and sunken; the waxen blade of his nose looked like a beak. He had long brown mustaches that hung straight down mournfully.*
*—from* LHA

> *He thought of the great barns of Pennsylvania, the ripe bending of golden grain, the plenty, the order, the clean thrift of the people. And he thought of how he had set out to get order and position for himself, and of the rioting confusion of his life, the blot and blur of years, and the red waste of his youth. "By God!" he thought. "I'm getting old! Why here?"—from* **LHA**

mother's people, the Penlands, were Carolinians who had distinguished themselves in both the French and Indian War and the American Revolution.

Julia was the fourth of eleven children born to Thomas Casey Westall by a second marriage (he had eight children by his first wife), in 1860, on the eve of the Civil War. She would always remember her childhood, with Reconstruction in full swing, as a time of anxiety and dire poverty. She described it as "the thorns and thistles of war, nothing but poverty, gloom, and sadness to remember. We all struggled on just to live, older people spent lots of time talking of what they had suffered, in loss of life and property—Negroes set free and all seemed to fear the Negro or what he might be persuaded to do. I remember lots of men and women would whisper, 'There are carpetbag-

THIS IS THE HOME THAT W. O. BUILT FOR CYNTHIA AT 92 WOODFIN STREET IN ASHEVILLE.

*He had little money, but his strange house grew to the rich modelling of his fantasy; when he had finished he had something which leaned to the slope of his narrow uphill yard, something with a high embracing porch in front, and warm rooms where one stepped up and down to the tackings of his whim. He built his house close to the quiet hilly street; he bedded the loamy soil with flowers; he laid the short walk to the high veranda steps with great square sheets of colored marble; he put a fence of spiked iron between his house and the world.—from* LHA

gers going among the Negroes and they may burn us up any night.' Every family had lost two to four young men in the Civil War."

She attended school only occasionally during her childhood, though she was later able to attend two "women's colleges," which today would be called high schools. But it was enough to qualify her to teach in a country school, and she supple-

mented her income by selling books door-to-door in Asheville.

In fact, it was while involved in this latter endeavor that she met her future husband, W.O. Wolfe.

---

For a more detailed account of W. O. Wolfe's early life, see Richard Walser's excellent work: *The Wolfe Family in Raleigh* (Raleigh: Wolf's Head Press, 1976).

JULIA WESTALL (CALLED ELIZA GANT IN *ANGEL*). BORN IN 1860, SHE WAS
TEACHING SCHOOL IN BAKERSVILLE WHEN THIS PHOTO WAS TAKEN IN 1884.

*Merciful God! he thought, with an anguished inner grin.  But she's a
pippin as sure as you're born.  He looked appreciatively at her trim
erect figure, noting her milky white skin, her black-brown eyes, with
their quaint child's stare, and her jet black hair drawn back tightly
from her high white forehead.  She had a curious trick of pursing her
lips reflectively before she spoke;  she liked to take her time, and came
to the point after interminable divagations down all the lane-ends of
memory and overtone, feasting upon the golden pageant of all she had
ever said, done, felt, thought, seen, or replied, with egocentric delight.*
—*from LHA*

Here the dapper W.O. is all frocked out in preparation for his wedding to Julia Westall in January of 1885.

Julia soon after her marriage to W.O. She was the daughter of industrious and sober Scotch-Irish Presbyterians and had little tolerance for W.O.'s drinking sprees. Sadly, she would outlive four of their eight children.

BACCHUS WESTALL, JULIA'S UNCLE, JOKINGLY CALLED
"THE PROPHET OF ARMAGEDDON."

*One day in April, as with fresh awakened senses, he stood before his shop, watching the flurry of life in the square, Oliver heard behind him the voice of a man who was passing. And that voice, flat, drawling, complacent, touched with sudden light a picture that had lain dead in him for twenty years.*

*"Hit's a comin'! According to my figgers hit's due June 11, 1896."*

*Oliver turned and saw retreating the burly persuasive figure of the prophet he had last seen vanishing down the dusty road that led to Gettysburg and Armageddon.*

*"Who is that man?" he asked a man.*

*The man looked and grinned.*

*"That's Bacchus Pentland," he said. "He's quite a character. There are a lot of his folks around here."*

*—from LHA*

JULIA'S MOTHER AND THE WIFE OF THOMAS WESTALL. SHE WAS A PENLAND BY BIRTH, FROM WHICH THOMAS WOLFE DERIVED THE NAME "PENTLAND" FOR THE WESTALLS IN *LOOK HOMEWARD, ANGEL*.

THOMAS CASEY WESTALL, THE GRANDFATHER FOR WHOM THOMAS WOLFE WAS NAMED. HE SERVED AS A MAJOR IN A NORTH CAROLINA MILITIA UNIT DURING THE CIVIL WAR AND BECAME A BUILDING CONTRACTOR IN LATER YEARS. HE WROTE POETRY, EDITED A TEMPERANCE NEWSPAPER, WAS SOMETHING OF A MYSTIC (LIKE ALL THE WESTALLS), AND EVENTUALLY BROKE AWAY FROM THE PRESBYTERIAN CHURCH OVER PREDESTINATION. IT IS SAID THAT, LIKE HIS FATHER BEFORE HIM, HE PREDICTED THE HOUR OF HIS OWN DEATH. W.O., WHO WAS DRIVEN TO DISTRACTION BY MAJOR WESTALL'S MYSTICAL AIR AND SELF-SATISFIED PIETY, DELIGHTED IN FREQUENTLY REFERRING TO HIM AS "THAT OLD HOG."

*The Pentland family was as old as any in the community, but it had always been poor, and had made few pretenses to gentility. By marriage, and by intermarriage among its own kinsmen, it could boast of some connection with the great, of some insanity, and a modicum of idiocy. But because of its obvious superiority in intelligence and fibre, to most of the mountain people it held a position of solid respect among them.*

*The Pentlands bore a strong clan-marking. Like most rich personalities in strange families their powerful group-stamp became more impressive because of their differences. They had broad powerful noses, with fleshy deeply scalloped wings, sensual mouths, extraordinarily mixed of delicacy and coarseness, which in the process of thinking they convolved with astonishing flexibility, broad intelligent foreheads, and deep flat cheeks, a trifle hollowed. The men were generally of ruddy face, and their typical stature was meaty, strong and of middling height, although it varied into gangling cadaverousness.—from* LHA

THE MARBLE SHOP AT 22 PACK SQUARE. HERE, SURROUNDED BY MARBLES, STANDS W.O. AND JULIA'S BROTHER, WILL WESTALL (CALLED WILL PENTLAND IN *ANGEL*), WITH WHOM W.O. HAD ENTERED INTO AN UNEASY PARTNERSHIP. NOTE THAT THE BEARDED GENTLEMAN STANDING ON THE UPPER DECK (TOP, RIGHT) IS JULIA'S FATHER, THOMAS WESTALL.

*"What's the matter with you, W.O.?" asked Will Pentland, looking up innocently from his fingers. "Had something to eat that didn't agree with you?"—he winked pertly at Duncan, and went back to his fingers.*

*"Your miserable old father," howled Gant, "was horsewhipped on the public square for not paying his debts." This was a purely imaginative insult, which had secured itself as truth, however, in Gant's mind, as had so many other stock epithets, because it gave him heart-cockle satisfaction.*

*"Horsewhipped upon the public square, was he?" Will winked again, unable to resist the opening. "They kept it mighty quiet, didn't they?" But behind the intense good-humored posture of his face, his eyes were hard. He pursed his lips meditatively as he worked upon his fingers.*

*"But I'll tell you something about him, W.O.," he continued after a moment, with calm but boding judiciousness. "He let his wife die a natural death in her own bed. He didn't try to kill her."*

*"No, by God!" Gant rejoined. "He let her starve to death. If the old woman ever got a square meal in her life she got it under my roof. There's one thing sure: she could have gone to Hell and back, twice over, before she got it from old Tom Pentland, or any of his sons."—from LHA*

TWO SHOTS OF PACK SQUARE CIRCA 1900, SHOWING DIFFERENT VIEWS OF W.O.'S MARBLE SHOP.

*The Square had the horrible concreteness of a dream. At the far southeastern edge he saw his shop—his name painted hugely in dirty scaly white across the brick near the roof: W.O. Gant—Marbles, Tombstones, Cemetery Fixtures. It was like a dream of hell, when a man finds his own name staring at him from the Devil's ledger; like a dream of death, when he who comes as mourner finds himself in the coffin, or as witness to a hanging, the condemned upon the scaffold.—from LHA*

JULIA AND BABY LESLIE, BORN IN 1885. SHE WOULD DIE WITHIN THE YEAR OF CHOLERA.

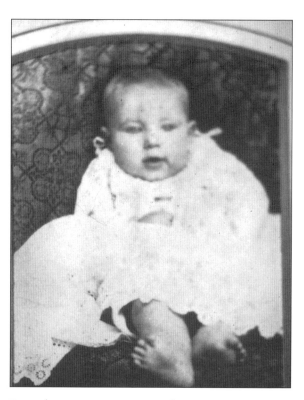

EFFIE (CALLED DAISY IN *ANGEL*), BORN IN 1887.

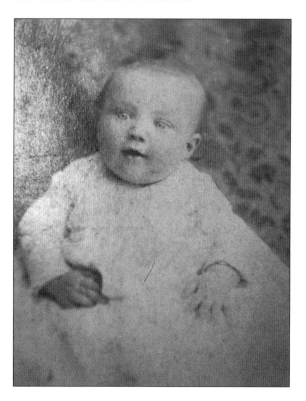

FRANK (CALLED STEVE IN *ANGEL*), BORN IN 1888.

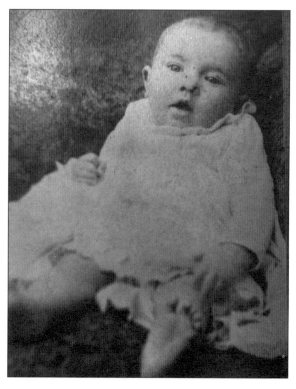

MABEL (CALLED HELEN IN *ANGEL*), BORN IN 1890.

THE TWINS, BORN IN 1892: THE FAIR BENJAMIN HARRISON WOLFE AND THE DARK, ILL-FATED GROVER CLEVELAND WOLFE.

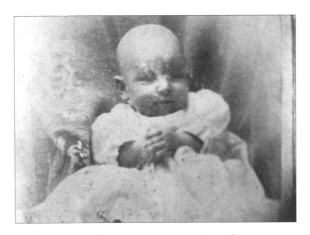

FRED WOLFE (CALLED LUKE IN *ANGEL*) MADE HIS APPEARANCE IN 1894.

*In eleven years she bore him nine children of whom six lived. The first, a girl, died in her twentieth month, of infant cholera; two more died at birth. The others outlived the grim and casual littering. The oldest, a boy, was born in 1885. He was given the name of Steve. The second, born fifteen months later, was a girl—Daisy. The next, likewise a girl—Helen—came three years later. Then, in 1892, came twin boys—to whom Gant, always with a zest for politics, gave the names of Grover Cleveland and Benjamin Harrison. The last, Luke, was born two years later, in 1894.—from* LHA

W.O.'S OLDER BROTHER, WESLEY WOLFE, AND HIS FAMILY. WESLEY ACCOMPANIED W.O. AND CYNTHIA FROM RALEIGH TO ASHEVILLE, WHERE HE WOULD IN TIME BECOME A PROSPEROUS BUILDING CONTRACTOR. (ONE NOTES THE STRONG RESEMBLENCE BETWEEN WESLEY AND W.O.)

JULIA WAS AN INVETERATE TRAVELER AND WOULD PACK UP HER CHILDREN AND FLY TO THE ENDS OF THE EARTH AT THE LEAST PRETEXT. HERE THEY POSE IN FRONT OF THE OLD SPANISH FORT IN ST. AUGUSTINE, FLORIDA ON MARCH 21, 1897. (L-R:) FRANK, JULIA, MABEL, EFFIE, BEN AND GROVER, AND FRED (IN THE WHITE SAILOR SUIT).

> *Once, Eliza and four of her children were sick at the same time with typhoid fever. But during a weary convalescence she pursed her lips grimly and took them off to Florida.—from LHA*

W.O. AND JULIA POSE PROUDLY IN THE YARD OF THE HOME THAT W.O. HAD BUILT FOR CYNTHIA AT 92 WOODFIN STREET. LINED UP ALONG THE PORCH RAILING ARE EFFIE, MABEL, FRANK, BEN AND GROVER, AND FRED. THIS PHOTO WAS MADE ABOUT 1899 AND CLEARLY ILLUSTRATES THAT THE COOL MOUNTAIN AIR HAD APPARENTLY DONE WONDERS TO CLEAR UP W.O.'S "IMPOTENCE."

# III

# THE EARLY YEARS
## (1900 - 1912)

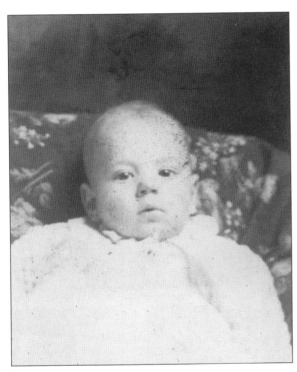 

THOMAS CLAYTON WOLFE (HIS MIDDLE NAME WAS DERIVED FROM A SPIRITUAL LECTURER WHOM JULIA GREATLY ADMIRED) WAS BORN ON OCTOBER 3, 1900. ACCORDING TO *ANGEL*, W.O. WAS IN THE FINAL THROES OF A GREAT DRUNK AT THE TIME OF TOM'S BIRTH AND, AFTER LOUDLY ACCUSING JULIA OF PROSTITUTING HERSELF ON THE STREETS OF ASHEVILLE, HE THREATENED THE LIFE OF BOTH HER AND HER OFFSPRING (FORTUNATELY HER BEDROOM DOOR WAS LOCKED IN ORDER TO AVOID JUST SUCH AN OCCURRENCE). IN REALITY, HOWEVER, W.O. WAS IN HIS FORTY-NINTH YEAR WHEN TOM WAS BORN AND WITHIN WEEKS OF HIS BIRTH THE PROUD W.O. WOULD EPITOMIZE THE DOTING FATHER, A ROLE HE WOULD PLAY UNTIL THE VERY END.

> *. . . a stone, a leaf, an unfound door; of a stone, a leaf, a door. And of all the forgotten faces.*
> *Naked and alone we came into exile. In her dark womb we did not know our mother's face; from the prison of her flesh have we come into the unspeakable and incommunicable prison of this earth.*
> *Which of us has known his brother? Which of us has looked into his father's heart? Which of us has not remained forever prison-pent? Which of us is not forever a stranger and alone?*
> *O waste of loss, in the hot mazes, lost, among bright stars on this most weary unbright cinder, lost! Remembering speechlessly we seek the great forgotten language, the lost lane-end into heaven, a stone, a leaf, an unfound door. Where? When?*
> *O lost, and by the wind grieved, ghost, come back again.—from LHA*

*So passed the winter. Eugene was three; they bought him alphabet books, and animal pictures, with rhymed fables below. Gant read them to him indefatigably; in six weeks he knew them all by memory. Through the late winter and spring he performed numberless times for the neighbors: holding the book in his hands he pretended to read what he knew by heart. Gant was delighted: he abetted the deception. Everyone thought it extraordinary that a child should read so young.—from* LHA

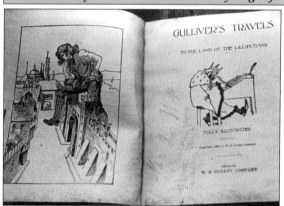

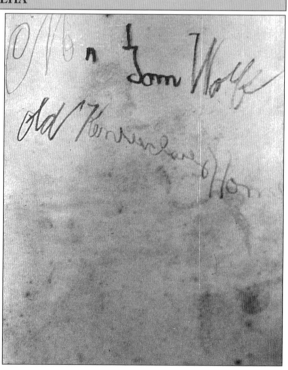

YOUNG TOM APPARENTLY AUTOGRAPHED THESE BOOK PAGES ABOUT 1906, SOON AFTER JULIA BOUGHT THE OLD KENTUCKY HOME. THESE BOOKS WERE IN THE POSSESSION OF EFFIE WOLFE GAMBRELL'S YOUNGEST SON, THE LATE ED GAMBRELL, OF ANDERSON, S.C. THEY ARE NOW A PART OF THE THOMAS WOLFE COLLECTION AT UNC.

IT WAS 1904 AND THE ENTERPRISING JULIA ANNOUNCED PLANS TO PACK UP THE CHILDREN AND HEAD FOR ST. LOUIS AND THE WORLD'S FAIR, WHERE SHE, IN HOPES OF PROFITING FROM A FLOURISHING TOURIST TRADE, HAD LEASED A ROOMING HOUSE CALLED THE NORTH CAROLINA AT 5095 FAIRMOUNT AVENUE. THE DEATH OF GROVER OF TYPHOID FEVER DURING THIS SOJOURN WOULD FOREVER HAUNT THE ENTIRE WOLFE FAMILY.

*And so at last he turned into the street, finding the place where the two corners met, the huddled block, the turret, and the steps, and paused a moment, looking back, as if the street were Time.*

*For a moment he stood there, waiting—for a word, and for a door to open, for the child to come. He waited, but no words were spoken; no one came.*

*Yet all of it was just as it had always been, except that the steps were lower, the porch less high, the strip of grass less wide, than he had thought. All the rest of it was as he had known it would be. A graystone front, three-storied, with a slant slate roof, the side red brick and windowed, still with the old arched entrance in the center for the doctor's use.—from* **The Lost Boy**

MABEL AT ABOUT THE TIME OF THE WORLD'S FAIR. ALREADY, AT THE AGE OF FOURTEEN, SHE WAS GROWING INTO THE BIG, SOMEWHAT HYSTERICAL WOMAN WHO WAS ALWAYS IN THE MIDDLE OF ALL FAMILY CONTROVERSIES. SHE WAS W.O.'S FAVORITE AND THE WORLD'S ONLY HUMAN BEING WHO COULD REASON WITH HIM WHEN HE WAS IN HIS CUPS.

M32006

THE HANDSOME FRANK AT THE AGE OF FIFTEEN IN 1904. HE WORKED A CONCESSION AT THE WORLD'S FAIR EACH DAY (AS DID GROVER) AND THIS WAS HIS PASS TO GAIN ENTRANCE.

*The boys worked on the Fair Grounds. They were call-boys at a place called the Inside Inn. —from* LHA

FRED, TEN YEARS OLD, STANDS TO THE REAR OF SEVERAL BOARDERS ON THE FRONT PORCH OF THE NORTH CAROLINA.

GROVER AND BEN.

*Sometimes, lying on a sunny quilt, Eugene grew conscious of a gentle peering face, a soft caressing voice, unlike any of the others in kind and quality, a tender olive skin, black hair, shoeblack eyes, exquisite, rather sad, kindliness. He nuzzled his soft face next to Eugene's, fondled and embraced him. On his brown neck he was birth-marked with a raspberry: Eugene touched it again and again with wonder. This was Grover—the gentlest and saddest of the boys.*
—*from* LHA

TOM WAS NOT QUITE FOUR DURING THE TRIP TO ST. LOUIS IN 1904, YET IN LATER YEARS HE WOULD SWEAR THAT HE STILL RETAINED VIVID MEMORIES OF GROVER AND THE ST. LOUIS ADVENTURE.

*He wondered what a cooling board was; the house was full of menace. Helen bore him out into the dimly lighted hall, and carried him to the rooms at the front of the house. Behind the door he heard low voices. Quietly she opened it; the light blazed brightly on the bed. Eugene looked, horror swarmed like poison through his blood. Behind the little wasted shell that lay there he remembered suddenly the warm brown face, the soft eyes, that once had peered down at him: like one who has been mad, and suddenly recovers reason, he remembered that forgotten face he had not seen in weeks, that strange bright loneliness that would not return. O lost, and by the wind grieved, ghost, come back again.*
—*from* LHA

In *The Lost Boy* Helen discusses Grover's death with Eugene, remarking that the above photo (taken July 4, 1899) reminds her of Time and the great changes wrought by Time. (L-R:) Effie, W.O., Mabel, Fred, Grover and Ben, Julia, and Frank.

*Didn't you ever see that picture of us? I was looking at it just the other day. It was made before the old house down on Woodson Street, with papa standing there in his swallow-tail, and mama there beside him—and Grover, and Ben, and Steve, and Daisy, and myself, with our feet upon our bicycles. Luke, poor kid, was only four or five. He didn't have a bicycle like us. But there he was. And there were all of us together.*

*Well, there I was, and my poor old skinny legs and long white dress, and two pigtails hanging down my back. And all the funny-looking clothes we wore, with the doo-lolly business on them. . . . But I guess you can't remember. You weren't born.*

*But, well, we were a right nice-looking set of people, if I do say so. And there was "86" the way it used to be, with the front porch, the grape vines, and the flower beds before the house—and "Miss Eliza" standing there by papa, with a watch charm pinned upon her waist. . . I shouldn't laugh, but "Miss Eliza"—well, mama was a pretty woman then. Do you know what I mean? "Miss Eliza" was a right good-looking woman, and papa in his swallow-tail was a good-looking man. Do you remember how he used to get dressed up on Sunday? And how grand we thought he was? And how he let me take his money out and count it? And how rich we thought he was? And how wonderful that dinkey little shop on the Square looked to us?*

*And there was Steve and Ben and Grover, Daisy, Luke, and me lined up there before the house with one foot on our bicycles. And I got to thinking back about it all. It all came back.*—from **The Lost Boy**

IN 1906, W.O. "THE FAR-WANDERER" SPENT TWO HAPPY WEEKS IN SAN FRANCISCO (HE IS STANDING AT THE REAR OF THE CARRIAGE), A TRIP TOM, IN HIS NOVEL, CALLS "GANT'S LAST GREAT VOYAGE."

*The journey to California was Gant's last great voyage. He made it two years after Eliza's return from St. Louis, when he was fifty-six years old. In the great frame was already stirring the chemistry of pain and death. Unspoken and undefined there was in him the knowledge that he was at length caught in the trap of life and fixity, that he was being borne under in this struggle against the terrible will that wanted to own the earth more than to explore it. This was the final flare of the old hunger that had once darkened in the small gray eyes, leading a boy into new lands and toward the soft stone smile of an angel.*—from **LHA**

THE INTERIOR OF W.O.'S MARBLE SHOP. JANNADEAU, THE SWISS WATCH REPAIRMAN WHO WAS FREQUENTLY CALLED ON TO HELP SUBDUE W.O. WHEN HE WAS ON ONE OF HIS DRINKING SPREES, IS STANDING AT THE FRONT LEFT IN THIS SHOT. THE DOUGHTY W.O. HIMSELF IS STANDING IN THE REAR.

In 1906, some two years after her return from St. Louis, Julia very shrewdly purchased the Old Kentucky Home (called Dixieland in *Angel*), much to the consternation of the proud W.O., who equated running a boardinghouse with taking in washing. But Julia would not be deterred. With six-year-old Tom under her wing, she fled 92 Woodfin, leaving W.O. and the other children to do as they pleased. This is where Tom grew up. Today it is on the National Register of Historic Places.

*Thus, she began to think of Dixieland. It was situated five minutes from the public square, on a pleasant sloping middle class street of small homes and boarding-houses. Dixieland was a big cheaply constructed frame house of eighteen or twenty drafty high-ceilinged rooms: it had a rambling, unplanned, gabular appearance, and was painted a dirty yellow. It had a pleasant green front yard, not deep but wide, bordered by a row of young deep-bodied maples: there was a sloping depth of one hundred and ninety feet, a frontage of one hundred and twenty. And Eliza, looking toward the town said: "They'll put a street behind there some day."*
—*from LHA*

WOLFE, WHO COULD BE THE LIFE OF THE PARTY ON OCCASIONS, SEEMED TO DERIVE DEEP PLEASURE THROUGHOUT HIS LIFE FROM CLOWNING AROUND IN HATS. THERE ARE NUMEROUS PHOTOS OF WOLFE IN FUNNY HATS, TAKEN MANY YEARS APART, WHICH ILLUSTRATE THIS POINT.

THIS FAMILY PHOTO WAS TAKEN AT 92 WOODFIN STREET ABOUT 1905. DESPITE THE FACT THAT W.O. AND ALL OF THE WOLFE CHILDREN (WITH THE EXCEPTION OF TOM) WOULD REMAIN HERE, THE OLD KENTUCKY HOME WOULD SOON BECOME THE CENTER OF FAMILY LIFE. (PICTURED HERE, IN DESCENDING ORDER:) MABEL, W.O., EFFIE, FRED, FRANK, JULIA, BEN, AND A WELL-BELTED BUT BAREFOOT TOM.

THE OLD KENTUCKY HOME, THE CENTER OF WOLFE FAMILY LIFE AFTER 1906.
(L-R:) W.O., BEN, JULIA, MABEL AND TOM.

By 1906, the year that Tom began attending the Orange Street School in Asheville, Julia was forty-six years old, W.O. fifty-five, and both elderly parents regarded young Tom as their darling plaything. This was particularly true of Julia, who nursed Tom until he was three and let him sleep in her bed until he was eight.

*He had won his first release from the fences of home—he was not quite six, when, of his own insistence, he went to school. Eliza did not want him to go, but his only close companion, Max Isaacs, a year his senior, was going, and there was in his heart a constricting terror that he would be left alone again. She told him he could not go: she felt, somehow, that school began the slow, the final loosening of the cords that held them together, but as she saw him slide craftily out the gate one morning in September and run at top speed to the corner where the other little boy was waiting, she did nothing to bring him back.—from* LHA

A SHOT TAKEN LATER IN LIFE OF MAX ISRAEL (CALLED MAX ISAACS IN *ANGEL*), TOM'S NEIGHBORHOOD CHUM, OF WHOM HE ENTERTAINED WARM MEMORIES. IT WAS MAX WHOM TOM FOLLOWED TO SCHOOL THAT FIRST FATEFUL DAY.

TOM, AT AGE SIX. EVEN AFTER HE ESCAPED JULIA'S GRASP TO ENROLL AT THE ORANGE STREET SCHOOL, SHE STILL REFUSED TO CUT HIS LONG BROWN LOCKS—MUCH TO TOM'S CHAGRIN.

*Eliza had allowed his hair to grow long; she wound it around her finger every morning into fat Fauntleroy curls; the agony and humiliation it caused him was horrible, but she was unable or unwilling to understand it, and mouth-pursingly thoughtful and stubborn to all solicitation to cut it . . . Even when his thick locks had become the luxuriant colony of Harry Tarkington's lice, she would not cut them: she held his squirming body between her knees twice a day and ploughed his scalp with a fine-toothed comb.—from* LHA

TOM AND HIS SECOND COUSIN MARY LOUISE WOLFE, THE GRANDDAUGHTER OF WESLEY WOLFE.

EFFIE (CALLED DAISY IN *ANGEL*) WAS BORN IN 1887 AND WAS THE OLDEST OF THE WOLFE CHILDREN. SHE FINISHED HIGH SCHOOL IN 1905 AND IN 1908 MARRIED FRED GAMBRELL (CALLED JOE GAMBEL IN *ANGEL*) OF ANDERSON, S.C. (CALLED HENDERSON IN *ANGEL*). THEREAFTER, FOR THE REST OF HIS LIFE, TOM WOULD LOOK FORWARD TO VISITS WITH EFFIE AND HER FAMILY AS A SPECIAL TREAT.

HERE IS EFFIE AT THE AGE OF SEVENTEEN. THIS PHOTO IS IN THE WOLFE FAMILY PHOTO ALBUM, LEAVING LITTLE DOUBT AS TO WHERE TOM DERIVED THE NAME DAISY FOR EFFIE IN *ANGEL*.

*She was seventeen and in her last year at high school. She was a timid, sensitive girl, looking like her name—Daisy-ish.*
*—from LHA*

EFFIE (TOP ROW, FAR RIGHT) WITH HER 1905 GRADUATING CLASS.

*Industrious and thorough in her studies, her teachers thought her one of the best students they had ever known. She had very little fire, or denial in her; she responded dutifully to instructions; she gave back what had been given to her. She played the piano without any passionate feeling for the music; but she rendered it honestly with a beautiful rippling touch. And she practiced hours at a time.—from LHA*

EFFIE IN 1908, AT ABOUT THE TIME OF HER MARRIAGE TO FRED GAMBRELL.

*Daisy had been married in the month of June following Eliza's purchase of Dixieland: the wedding was arranged on a lavish scale, and took place in the big dining-room of the house. Gant and his two older sons grinned sheepishly in unaccustomed evening dress. The Pentlands, faithful in their attendance at weddings and funerals, sent gifts and came. Will and Pett gave a heavy set of carving steels.*

*Thus Daisy passed more or less definitely out of Eugene's life, although he was to see her briefly on visits.—from* LHA

FRED GAMBRELL, THE SOMEWHAT PROVINCIAL JOE GAMBEL OF *LOOK HOMEWARD, ANGEL.*

*She had promised herself to a young South Carolinian, who was connected rather vaguely with the grocery trade. His hair was parted in the middle of his low forehead, his voice was soft, drawling, amiable, his manner hearty and insistent, his habits large and generous. He brought Gant cigars on his visits, the boys large boxes of assorted candies. Every one felt that he had favorable prospects.*

*"There's no place like Henderson," said he, with complacent and annoying fidelity, referring to that haven of enervation, red clay, ignorance, slander and superstition, in whose effluent rays he had been reared.—from* LHA

Oct. 23, 1908
Dear Effie,

I am sorry to hear you
are sick.

Mabel went to anderson this
morning.

It has been raining hear for two of
ther days.

I got your letter the other day.
If you don't get any better write
us and we will come down to see you.
I am getting of to school
in time every morning.
And I am never late.
I want to see you very much.
We have got the house cleaned fine

YOUNG TOM WROTE THE FOLLOWING TWO LETTERS TO EFFIE IN 1908 AND 1909, PERHAPS HIS EARLIEST LITERARY EFFORTS.
FRED SAYS THAT IT WAS TOM'S DELIGHT TO BOARD THE TRAIN IN ASHEVILLE FOR THE LONG RIDE TO ANDERSON ON THE
WEEKENDS, AND THAT TOM DERIVED THE NAME GANT FROM A LITTLE WAY STATION NEAR ANDERSON WHERE THE
PASSENGERS WOULD STOP FOR A PICNIC AND RECREATION. (IN 1975 THESE LETTERS WERE IN THE POSSESSION OF TOM'S
NEPHEW, ED GAMBRELL. MR. GAMBRELL IS NOW DECEASED.)

down at 92.

But we cant get papa to go.*

But Mama says soon as it

stops raining she is going to move

us down there any way.

I had better close my letter

now.

It is time for me to go to bed.

Good by,

Your little brother

Tom Wolfe

P.S.  Tell Fred I will write

him a letter next time.

---

*This refers to Julia's purchase of
the Old Kentucky Home and
W.O.'s refusal to leave 92 Woodfin
for what he termed "that dark and
bloody barn."

May 1909

Dear Effie

How are you feeling?
I am selling post and won a
prize last month and think
I am going to win won this month.*
I sold 61 post this weekend.
Fred is going to give the boy who
sell the most post this week 5 cents.
but I aint in it if I was I
would beat them all to pieces
so he don't want me in it the boys
would not feel like working if I
beat them.

We are going to have a peretty
good crop of fruit this year.
We will get out of school in two
or three weeks.

Goodby,

Your brother

Tom

_____

*Much of this letter concerns Tom's going out
on Saturdays to hawk the Saturday Evening
Post for Fred, who owned the franchise in
the Asheville area. Despite his boasts to Effie,
Tom was a most reluctant sales agent.

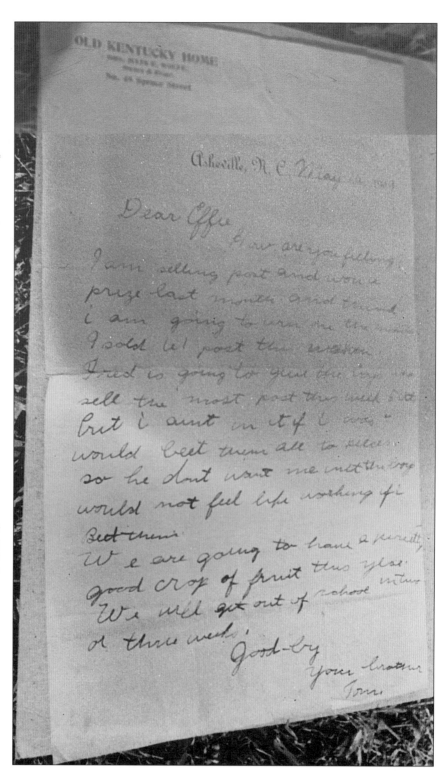

FRANK, MUCH MALIGNED AS STEVE IN *LOOK HOMEWARD, ANGEL,* AT ABOUT THE TIME OF EFFIE'S WEDDING. HE APPARENTLY DID EXPERIENCE SOME PROBLEMS AS A YOUNGSTER, BUT JULIA CLAIMED THAT THOSE PROBLEMS AROSE BECAUSE IT WAS HIS RESPONSIBILITY, AS THE ELDEST SON, EVEN AS A CHILD, TO HAUNT THE BARROOMS AND BAWDYHOUSES OF ASHEVILLE IN SEARCH OF HIS ERRING FATHER.

IT MIGHT BE NOTED THAT OF ALL THE WOLFE OFFSPRING, FRANK WAS THE ONLY ONE TO PRODUCE A CHILD WITH THE SURNAME WOLFE. DR. DIETZ WOLFE IS TODAY A NOTED PHYSICIAN IN LOUISVILLE.

BEN BY 1906 WAS FOURTEEN YEARS OLD AND ALREADY EARNING A REPUTATION IN THE WOLFE FAMILY AS "THE QUIET ONE." HE WAS SILENT, MOODY, AND INTENSE. YET, WITH TOM, HE COULD BE VERY GENEROUS AND OUTGOING. FIERCELY INDEPENDENT, HE QUIT SCHOOL AT THE AGE OF FOURTEEN TO TAKE A JOB IN THE CIRCULATION DEPARTMENT OF *THE ASHEVILLE CITIZEN.* TOM ALWAYS FELT A SPIRITUAL KINSHIP WITH BEN THAT HE EXPERIENCED WITH NONE OF HIS OTHER SIBLINGS. BEN WOULD DIE OF PNEUMONIA DURING THE FLU EPIDEMIC OF 1918.

> *It was apparent, however, that Steve was lacking in scholarship. When he was fourteen, he was summoned by the school principal to his little office to take a thrashing for truancy and insubordination. But the spirit of acquiescence was not in him; he snatched the rod from the man's hand, broke it, smote him solidly in the eye, and dropped gleefully eighteen feet to the ground.*
>
> *This was one of the best things he ever did: his conduct in other directions was less fortunate.*
>
> *Of them all, he had had very much the worst of it. Since his childhood he had been the witness of his father's wildest debauches. He had not forgotten.*
> —*from* **LHA**

> *He had aqueous gray eyes, and a sallow bumpy skin. His head was shapely, the forehead high and bony. His hair was crisp, maple-brown. Below his perpetual scowl, his face was small, converging to a point; his extraordinarily sensitive mouth smiled briefly, flickeringly, inwardly—like a flash of light along a blade. And he always gave a cuff instead of a caress; he was full of pride and tenderness.*
> —*from* **LHA**

BEN (TOP ROW, FAR RIGHT) AND THE NEWSBOYS OF *THE ASHEVILLE CITIZEN*.

*By this time Ben, sullen, silent, alone, had withdrawn more closely than ever into his heart: in the brawling house he came and went, and was remembered, like a phantom. Each morning at three o'clock, when his fragile unfurnished body should have been soaked in sleep, he got up under the morning stars, departed silently from the sleeping house, and went down to the roaring morning presses and the inksmell that he loved, to begin the delivery of his route. Almost without consideration by Gant and Eliza he slipped quietly away from school after the eighth grade, took on extra duties at the paper's office and lived, in sufficient bitter pride, upon his earnings. He slept at home, ate perhaps one meal a day there, loping home gauntly at night, with his father's stride, his thin long shoulders bent prematurely by the weight of the heavy paper bag, pathetically, hungrily Gantian.*—from LHA

ONE OF BEN'S DUTIES WAS TO MAN THIS BASEBALL SCOREBOARD MOUNTED OUTSIDE THE *CITIZEN'S* BUILDING. ANOTHER EMPLOYEE SAT JUST INSIDE THE WINDOW, HIS TELEGRAPH PICKING UP A MAJOR LEAGUE BASEBALL GAME. HE WOULD DESCRIBE THE GAME TO BEN, WHO WOULD THEN GIVE HUNDREDS OF EXCITED SPECTATORS A BLOW-BY-BLOW ACCOUNT OF THE GAME BY MOVING PLAYERS AROUND ON THE BOARD.

*He bore encysted within him the evidence of their tragic fault: he walked alone in the darkness, death and the dark angels hovered, and no one saw him. At three-thirty in the morning, with his loaded bag beside him, he sat with other route boys in a lunch room, with a cup of coffee in one hand and a cigarette in the other, laughing softly, almost noiselessly, with his flickering exquisitely sensitive mouth, his scowling gray eyes.*
—*from* **LHA**

FRED (BOTTOM ROW, THIRD FROM RIGHT) IS DEPICTED HERE WITH THE HIGH SCHOOL MINSTRELS. HE WAS SIX YEARS TOM'S SENIOR AND TOM'S SELF-APPOINTED MENTOR IN ALL MATTERS. HE WAS MABEL'S CONSTANT ALLY IN EVERY FAMILY CONTROVERSY AND WOULD SURVIVE HIS SIBLINGS BY MANY YEARS, DYING AT THE AGE OF EIGHTY-SIX.

He was Luke, the unique, Luke the incomparable: he was, in spite of his garrulous and fidgeting nervousness, an intensely likable person—and he really had in him a bottomless well of affection. He wanted bounteous praise for his acts, but he had a deep, genuine kindliness and tenderness.

Eugene remembered the soft cool nights of summer, the assembled boarders and "I Wonder Who's Kissing Her Now," which Gant demanded over and over; "Love Me and the World Is Mine"; Till the Sands of the Desert Grow Cold;" "Dear Old Girl;" "The 'Rob-bin Sings Above You;" "The End of a Perfect Day;" and "Alexander's Rag-Time Band," which Luke had practised in a tortured house for weeks, and sung with thunderous success in the High School Minstrels.—from LHA

MABEL, BORN IN 1890, WAS BY 1906 A YOUNG LADY OF SIXTEEN. ALWAYS TOTALLY IMMERSED IN WHATEVER CRISIS WAS BESETTING THE FAMILY AT THE MOMENT, SHE WAS W.O.'S PET AND INVARIABLY MADE IT A POINT TO CHAMPION HIS CAUSE, USUALLY AGAINST JULIA. SHE WAS CONSIDERED AN ACCOMPLISHED PIANIST AND VOCALIST, AND IN 1913 SHE AND A FRIEND WOULD FORM A DUET AND GO ON TOUR, ENTERTAINING AUDIENCES IN SMALL THEATERS ACROSS THE SOUTH. HER ATTITUDE TOWARDS TOM, AS IN MOST OTHER MATTERS, WAS SOMEWHAT AMBIGUOUS. SHE COULD BE HIS LOVING ADVOCATE ONE MOMENT, HIS SNARLING CRITIC THE NEXT.

*She was almost six feet tall: she had large hands and feet, thin straight legs, a big-boned generous face, with the long full chin slightly adroop, revealing her big gold-traced upper teeth. But, in spite of this gauntness, she did not look hard-featured or raw-boned. Her face was full of heartiness and devotion, sensitive, whole-souled, hurt, bitter, hysterical, but at times transparently radiant and handsome.*
*—from LHA*

MABEL IN HER THEATRICAL COSTUME. SHE WAS A LIVELY EXTROVERT, AND, LIKE FRED, SHE THRIVED ON APPLAUSE.

*Like Gant, like Luke, Helen needed extension in life, movement, excitement: she wanted to dominate, to entertain, to be the life of the party. On small solicitation, she sang for the boarders, thumping the cheap piano with her heavy accurate touch, and singing in her strong, vibrant, somewhat hard soprano a repertory of songs, classical, sentimental and comic.—from LHA*

A STRIP OF PENNY ARCADE PHOTOS SHOWING MABEL FROM DIFFERENT ANGLES.

PEARL SHOPE (CALLED PEARL HINES IN *ANGEL*), MABEL'S SINGING PARTNER.

*Pearl Hines, daughter of a Baptist saddle-maker: she was heavy of body and face, but she had a powerful rag-time singing voice.—from* LHA

MABEL WOLFE AND PEARL SHOPE. THEY BILLED
THEMSELVES AS "WOLFE AND SHOPE: SINGERS FROM
RAG-TIME TO OPERA" (CALLED THE DIXIE MELODY
TWINS IN *ANGEL*). TOGETHER THEY THRILLED AUDIENCES
FOR ALMOST TWO YEARS, 1913-14.

*In these years Helen went off into the South
with Pearl Hines, the saddlemaker's daughter.
They sang together at moving-picture theatres
in country towns. They were booked from a
theatrical office in Atlanta.*

    *Pearl Hines was a heavily built girl with a
meaty face and negroid lips. She was jolly and
vital. She sang rag-time and nigger songs with a
natural passion, swinging her hips and shaking
her breasts erotically.—from* LHA

MABEL NEGOTIATES A FEE WITH THE MANAGER OF THE ELKS THEATER IN NEW IBERIA, LOUISIANA.

Tom and Julia in 1910. Tom had grown into a handsome youngster, and, despite some initial misgivings, had become one of the most successful paper boys ever to sling a daily for *The Asheville Citizen*. He had also become Julia's trusted traveling companion on her vacations throughout the Southeast.

Tom and Julia, along with other guests, at a boardinghouse in Hot Springs, Arkansas, 1910.

*Eliza sent him to one of the public schools of Hot Springs: he plunged heavily into the bewildering new world—performed brilliantly and won the affection of the woman who taught him, but paid the penalty of the stranger to all the hostile and banded little creatures of the class. Before his first month was out, he had paid desperately for his ignorance of their customs.—from* LHA

The two shots on this page are interesting, though the occasions remain a mystery. The top photo was taken at the Old Kentucky Home about 1910 and shows Fred (top, third from left), Frank (bottom, second from left), and Tom (bottom, right).

In the second photo, apparently taken the same day as the first, Frank is depicted with his future wife, Margaret Dietze (kneeling behind Frank's left shoulder), then Ben (with hat) and Tom.

Tom (bottom row, far left) as a fifth grader at the Orange Street School in 1910. The teacher is Miss Bessie Moody (called Miss Groody in *Angel*—"*Old Miss Groody has Good Toody.*")

*He was now in one of the upper grades of grammar school, he was one of the Big Boys. His hair had been cut when he was nine years old, after a bitter siege against Eliza's obstinacy. He no longer suffered because of the curls. But he had grown like a weed, he already topped his mother by an inch or two; his body was big-boned but very thin and fragile, with no meat on it; his legs were absurdly long, thin, and straight, giving him a curious scissored look as he walked with long bounding strides.—from* LHA

A detail from the above photo.

This photo was taken about 1910. (L-R:) Ben, Fred, Tom, Julia and two boarders at the Old Kentucky Home.

*He was almost twelve. He was done with childhood.
As that Spring ripened he felt entirely, for the first
time, the full delight of loneliness. Stuck on a thin
undeveloped neck beneath a big wide-browed head
covered thickly by curling hair which had changed,
since his infancy, from a light maple to dark brown-
black, was a face so small, and so delicately
sculptured, that it seemed not to belong to its body.
The strangeness, the remote quality of this face was
enhanced by its brooding fabulous concentration, by
its passionate dark intensity, across which every
splinter of thought or sensation flashed like a streak
of light across a pool. His rapt dreaming intensity set
the face usually in an expression of almost sullen
contemplation.—from LHA*

# THE NORTH STATE YEARS

## (1912 - 1916)

Tom enrolled in the North State Fitting School on Buxton Hill in 1912. John Roberts (called John Leonard in *Angel*), the headmaster, had formerly served as principal at the Orange Street School and was so impressed with Tom's intellectual abilities that he implored Julia and W.O. to pay for Tom to enroll at the new school. After some deliberation, they did.

*Mr. Leonard had leased an old pre-war house, set on a hill wooded by magnificient trees. It faced west and south, looking toward Biltburn, and abruptly down on South End, and the negro flats that stretched to the depot.*
*—from LHA*

MARGARET ROBERTS (CALLED MARGARET LEONARD IN *ANGEL*), TOM'S TEACHER AT NORTH STATE. IN LATER YEARS HE WOULD CALL HER "THE MOTHER OF MY SPIRIT."

> *Her thin face was given a touch of shrewdness of decision by the straight line of her nose, the fine long carving of her chin. Beneath the sallow minutely pitted skin in her cheeks, and about her mouth, several frayed nerve-centers twitched from moment to moment, jarring the skin slightly without contorting or destroying the passionate calm beauty that fed her inexhaustibly from within.*
>
> *She did not have knowledge. But she had wisdom. She found immediately a person's quality. Boys were her heroes, her little gods. She believed that the world was to be saved, life redeemed, by one of them. She saw the flame that burns in each of them, and she guarded it. She tried somehow to reach the dark gropings toward light and articulation, of the blunt, the stolid, the shamefast. She spoke a calm low word to the trembling racehorse, and he was still.—from* LHA

JOHN AND MARGARET ROBERTS AND THEIR TWO CHILDREN, BUDDY AND MARGARET.

> *Margaret Leonard at this time was thirty-four years old. She had borne two children, a son who was now six years old, and a daughter who was two. She was of middling height, five feet six inches perhaps. As the giddiness of his embarrassment wore off he saw that she could not weigh more than eighty or ninety pounds. He had heard of the children. Now he remembered them, and Leonard's white muscular bulk, with a sense of horror. His swift vision leaped at once to the sexual relation, and something in him twisted aside, incredulous and afraid.—from* LHA

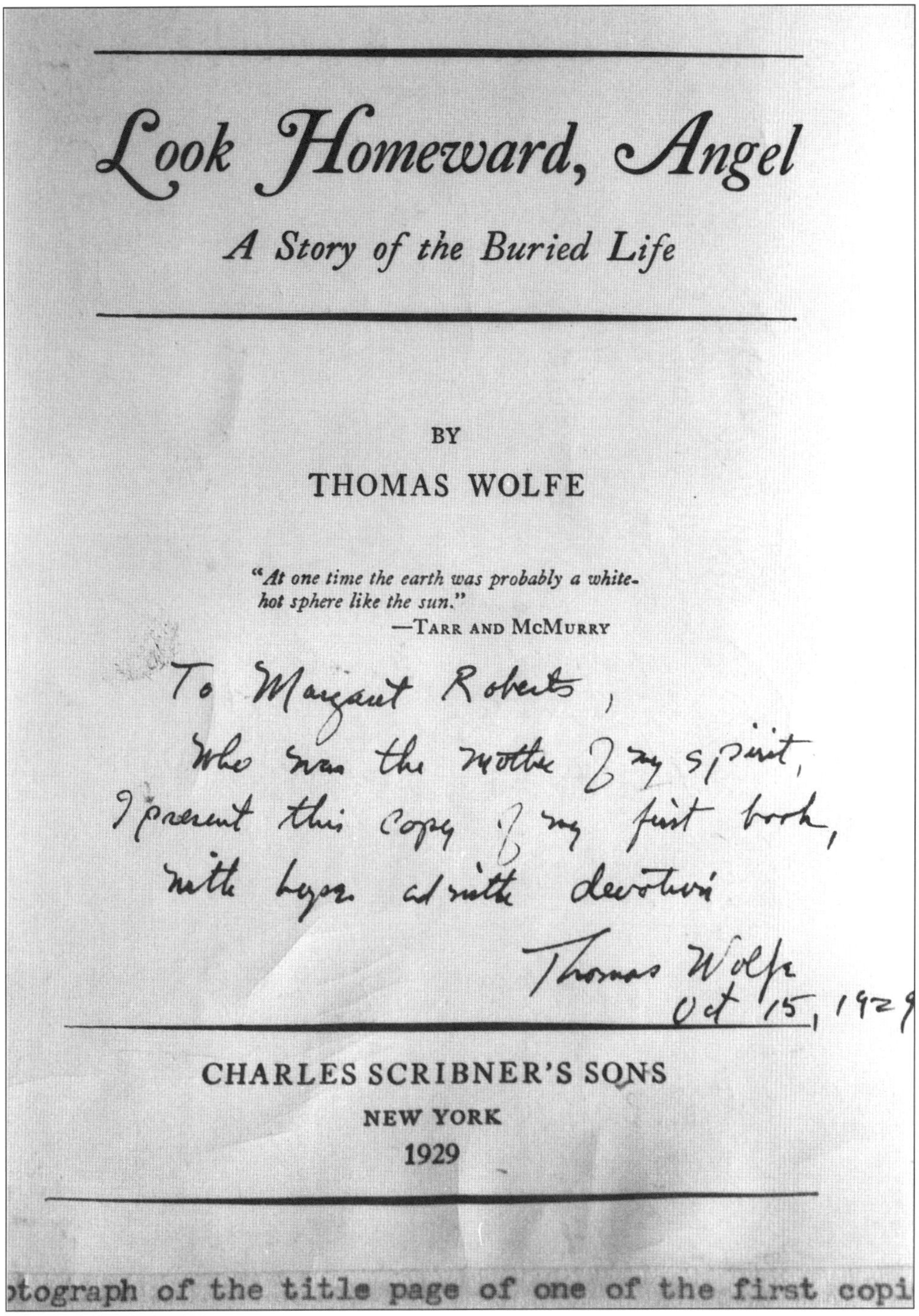

Look Homeward, Angel

A Story of the Buried Life

BY

THOMAS WOLFE

"*At one time the earth was probably a white-hot sphere like the sun.*"
—TARR AND McMURRY

To Margaret Roberts,
who was the mother of my spirit,
I present this copy of my first book,
with love and with devotion

Thomas Wolfe
Oct 15, 1929

CHARLES SCRIBNER'S SONS
NEW YORK
1929

otograph of the title page of one of the first copi

THE TITLE PAGE FROM *LOOK HOMEWARD, ANGEL* THAT TOM PRESENTED TO MARGARET ROBERTS IN 1929.

Tom as a hail-fellow-well-met student at the North State in 1915. (L-R:) Henry Harris, Tom, Joe Taylor, Julius Martin, Junius Horner, Reid Russell, and John Roberts.

The handsome Frank at about the time of his marriage to Margaret Dietze.

FRANK MARRIED MARGARET DIETZE (CALLED MARGARET LUTZ IN *ANGEL*), DAUGHTER OF A WEALTHY MANUFACTURER FROM NEW ALBANY, INDIANA. HERE THEY ARE WITH THEIR SON, DIETZ WOLFE.

*It was a period of incessant movement in the family. Steve had married a year or two before a woman from a small town in lower Indiana. She was thirty-seven years old, twelve years his senior, a squat heavy German with a big nose and a patient and ugly face. She had come to Dixieland one summer with another woman, a spinster of lifelong acquaintance, and allowed him to seduce her before she left. The winter following, her father, a small manufacturer of cigars, had died, leaving her $9,000 in insurance, his home, a small sum of money in the bank, and a quarter share in his business, which was left to the management of his two sons.*
—from **LHA**

IN 1912 FRED WOLFE ENROLLED IN A TOUGH ENGINEERING PROGRAM AT GEORGIA TECH. SOCIABLE AND FRIENDLY, FRED WAS TWICE ELECTED BY THE STUDENT BODY TO DELIVER THE FUNERAL ORATION OVER THE UNIVERSITY OF GEORGIA FOLLOWING THEIR ANNUAL FOOTBALL GAME. HERE, DRESSED AS A MORTICIAN, FRED STANDS BESIDE THE OLD WOODEN FENCE AT GRANT FIELD AWAITING THE KICKOFF. HE WOULD REMAIN AT TECH FOR THREE YEARS BEFORE GIVING IT UP AND RETURNING HOME. IN 1926, HOWEVER, AT THE AGE OF THIRTY-TWO, FRED WOULD FINALLY GRADUATE FROM GEORGIA TECH WITH A DEGREE IN ELECTRICAL ENGINEERING.

> *Luke worked as hard for an education as any other self-made man. He made every sacrifice. He did everything but study.*
>
> *He was an immense popular success, so very extra, so very Lukey. The school sought and adored him. Twice, after football games, he mounted a hearse and made funeral orations over the University of Georgia.*
>
> *But, in spite of all his effort, toward the end of his third year he was still a sophomore with every prospect of remaining one.*
>
> *He was not an electrical engineer—he was electrical energy.—from LHA*

THE HANDSOME FRED.

*Enormous humor flowed from him like crude light. Men who had never known him seethed with strange internal laughter when they saw him, and roared helplessly when he began to speak. Yet, his physical beauty was astonishing. His head was like that of a wild angel—coils and whorls of living golden hair flashed from his head, his features were regular, generous, and masculine, illuminated by the strange inner smile of idiot ecstacy.—from* LHA

FRED TAKES AN UNIDENTIFIED FRIEND OUT FOR A SPIN IN W.O.'S NEW 1913 FORD.

*Otherwise, he drove Gant's car—a 1913 five-passenger Ford, purchase of an inspired hour of madness, occupant now of half Gant's conversation, object of abuse, boast, and anathema.—from* LHA

FRED'S LOVE AFFAIR WITH W.O.'S CAR WAS LEGEND IN ASHEVILLE, AS WAS
HIS LACK OF DRIVING SKILLS.

*Luke drove nervously, erratically, wildly—his stammering impatient
hands and knees communicated their uneven fidget to the flivver. He
cursed irritably, plunged in exacerbated fury at the brake, and burst out
in an annoyed tuh-tuh-tuh-tuh when the car stalled.*

*"You Goddamned scoundrel!" Gant yelled. "Stop you mountain grill,
or I'll put you in jail."*

*"What-whah-whah." His laughter soared to a crazy falsetto.*

*Daisy, arrived for a few weeks of summer coolness, quite blue with
terror, would clutch the most recent of her annual arrivals to her breast,
melodramatically, and moan:*

*"I beg of you, for the sake of my family, for the sake of my innocent
motherless babes!"*

*"Whah-whah-whah!"—from LHA*

W.O. AT SIXTY-FIVE: STILL A HANDSOME MAN, PROSPEROUS, AND WELL RESPECTED IN THE COMMUNITY DESPITE AN OCCASIONAL PECCADILLO.

*One afternoon in the young summer, Gant leaned upon the rail, talking to Jannadeau. He was getting on to sixty-five, his erect body had settled, he stooped a little. He spoke of old age often, and he wept in his tirades now because of his stiffened hand. Soaked in pity, he referred to himself as "the poor old cripple who has to provide for them all."—from* LHA

IT'S GENERALLY HELD THAT, THIS IS THE ANGEL THAT STOOD ON W.O.'S FRONT PORCH AND THE ONE WOLFE HAD IN MIND WHEN HE WROTE *ANGEL*. BUT ACCORDING TO WOLFE SCHOLAR TED MITCHELL W.O. SOLD SOME FIFTEEN SUCH ANGELS BETWEEN 1905 AND 1915, AND THUS THE ANGEL WOLFE HAD IN MIND COULD VERY WELL BE A COMPOSITE OF SEVERAL ANGELS.

REGARDLESS, IN THE NOVEL W.O. RELUCTANTLY SELLS HIS ANGEL TO QUEEN ELIZABETH, OWNER OF AN ALTAMONT BAWDYHOUSE, TO PLACE OVER THE GRAVE OF ONE OF HER RECENTLY DECEASED WORKING GIRLS.

*His face was shocked and unwilling. He gnawed the corner of his thin lip. No one knew how fond he was of the angel. Publicly he called it his White Elephant. He cursed it and said he had been a fool to order it. For six years it had stood on the porch, weathering, in all the wind and the rain. It was now brown and fly-specked. But it had come from Carrara in Italy, and it held a stone lily delicately in one hand. The other hand was lifted in benediction, it was poised clumsily upon the ball of one phthisic foot, and its stupid white face wore a smile of soft stone idiocy.*

*In his rages, Gant sometimes directed vast climaxes of abuse at the angel. "Fiend out of Hell!" he roared. "You have impoverished me, you have ruined me, you have cursed my declining years, and now you will crush me to death, fearful, awful, and unnatural monster that you are."*

*But sometimes when he was drunk he fell weeping on his knees before it, called it Cynthia, and entreated its love, forgiveness, and blessing for its sinful but repentant boy. There was laughter from the Square.*

*"What's the matter?" said Elizabeth. "Don't you want to sell it?"*

*"It will cost you a good deal, Elizabeth," he said evasively.*

*"I don't care," she answered, positively. "I've got the money. How much do you want?"—from* LHA

THE BEAUTIFUL ANNIE HARPER OSBORNE (CALLED MRS. SELBORNE IN *ANGEL*), ANOTHER NATIVE OF ANDERSON, S.C. IN THE NOVEL, BEN IS QUITE TAKEN WITH MRS. SELBORNE.

THE NOTORIOUS PLAYHOUSE AT 92 WOODFIN STREET, WHERE A TIPSY W.O., ASSUMING THAT HE WAS ALL ALONE, ATTEMPTED TO INITIATE AN INTIMATE AFFAIR WITH MRS. SELBORNE'S MAID. UNFORTUNATELY FOR W.O., THE OUTRAGED MAID REFUSED TO COOPERATE AND IN FACT SPILLED THE BEANS TO A FURIOUS MABEL. THIS EVENT BECAME ONE OF W.O.'S MOST HUMILIATING MISADVENTURES.

*For some weeks now it had been occupied by Mrs. Selborne's South Carolina cook, Annie, a plump comely negress of thirty-five, with a rich coppery skin.*

*That morning, Gant had wakened earlier and stared at his ceiling thoughtfully. He had risen, dressed, and wearing his leather slippers, walked softly back, along the boards, to the playhouse. Helen was roused by Annie's loud protests. Tingling with premonition she came down stairs and found Gant wringing his hands and moaning as he walked up and down the washroom. Through the open doors she heard the negress complaining loudly to herself as she banged out drawers and slammed her belongings together.*

*"I ain't used to no such goins-on. I'se a married woman, I is. I ain't goin' to stay in dis house anothah minnit."*
*—from LHA*

MABEL AND HER FIANCE, RALPH WHEATON (CALLED HUGH BARTON IN *ANGEL*), AN EMPLOYEE OF THE NATIONAL CASH REGISTER CO. HE WAS A NATIVE OF TOLEDO, OHIO, BUT HE WAS LIVING IN ANDERSON, S.C. (CALLED HENDERSON IN *ANGEL*) AT THE TIME HE AND MABEL MET. EFFIE AND FRED, COINCIDENTALLY, ALSO FOUND SPOUSES IN ANDERSON.

> *She had returned to Altamont in May, from her last singing engagement. She had been in Atlanta for the week of opera, and had come back by way of Henderson, where she had visited Daisy and Mrs. Selborne. There she had found her mate.*
>
> *He was not a stranger to her. She had known him years before in Altamont, where he had lived for a short time as district agent for the great and humane corporation that employed him—The Federal Cash Register Company.—from LHA*

MABEL AND RALPH IN 1918.

MABEL AND RALPH WERE MARRIED AT THE OLD KENTUCKY HOME ON JUNE 28, 1916. (L-R:) EUGENIA BROWN, TOM, THELMA OSBORNE, MRS. C.A. WHEATON, MIRIAM GAMBRELL, GERALDINE NORTON (RALPH'S SISTER), FRED, PEARL SHOPE, RALPH WHEATON, MABEL, EFFIE, BEN, SARAH LEE BROWN, JULIA, W.O., ANNIE HARPER OSBORNE, AND FRED GAMBRELL.

*Ferns, flowers, potted plants, presents and guests arriving. The long nasal drone of the Presbyterian minister. The packed crowd. The triumphant booming of The Wedding March.*

*A flashlight: Hugh Barton and his bride limply astare—frightened; Gant, Ben, Luke, and Eugene, widely, sheepishly agrin; Eliza, high-sorrowful and sad; Mrs. Selborne and a smile of subtle mystery; the pert flower-girls; Pearl Hines' happy laughter.—from* LHA

Tom at the time of Mabel's wedding. He had three older brothers of wildly varying personalities, and he unconsciously tried to emulate the best qualities of each, creating for himself among the more solid citizens of Asheville a reputation of high middle–class respectability, an image he studiously disavows in *Angel*.

> *He was not so attractive physically—he had lost the round contours of infancy, he had grown up like a weed, his limbs were long and gangling, his feet large, his shoulders bony, and his head too big and heavy for the scrawny neck on which it sagged forward.—from* **LHA**

THE WEDDING PHOTO. (L-R:) JULIA, W.O., ANNIE HARPER OSBORNE, AND FRED GAMBRELL.

MIRIAM GAMBRELL, EFFIE'S DAUGHTER AND ONE OF THE "PERT FLOWER GIRLS" IN *ANGEL*.

MRS. C. A. WHEATON, RALPH WHEATON'S MOTHER (CALLED MRS. BARTON IN *ANGEL*). SHE DID IN FACT BECOME ILL WITH VOMITING AND DIARRHEA IMMEDIATELY FOLLOWING THE WEDDING, AND HER ILLNESS DID DELAY MABEL AND RALPH'S HONEYMOON TRIP TO NIAGARA FALLS FOR OVER A WEEK. TOM IS NOT KIND TO HER IN *ANGEL*.

*Hugh Barton's mother was in her seventy-fourth year, but she had the strength of a healthy woman of fifty, and the appetite of two of forty. She was a powerful old lady, six feet tall, with the big bones of a man, equipped with a champing mill of strong yellow horse-teeth. It was cake and pudding to see her at work on corn on the cob. A slight paralysis had slowed her tongue and thickened her speech a little, so that she spoke deliberately, with a ponderous enunciation of each word. This deformity, which she carefully hid, added to, rather than subtracted from, the pontifical weight of her opinions: she was an earnest Republican—in memory of her departed mate—and she took a violent dislike to any one who opposed her political judgement. When thwarted or annoyed in any way, the heavy benevolence of her face was dislodged by a thunder-cloud of petulance, and her wide pouting underlip rolled out like a window-shade.—from* LHA

TOM (IN MIDDLE, WITH ARMS FOLDED) WITH HIS FELLOW STUDENTS AT THE NORTH STATE FITTING SCHOOL FROM WHICH HE GRADUATED IN JUNE OF 1916. BECAUSE OF TOM'S YOUTH (HE WAS ONLY FIFTEEN) JOHN ROBERTS APPEALED TO W.O. TO PERMIT TOM TO REMAIN IN SCHOOL FOR ONE MORE YEAR. BUT W.O. WAS ADAMANT: NO MORE MONEY WOULD GO TO NORTH STATE, TOM WAS READY FOR COLLEGE. AS FOR TOM, HE HAD HIS HEART SET ON ATTENDING THE UNIVERSITY OF VIRGINIA, BUT W.O. WAS AGAIN ADAMANT: IT WAS THE UNIVERSITY OF NORTH CAROLINA OR NOWHERE.

*"He's ready to go," said Gant, "and he's going to the State University, and nowhere else. He'll be given as good an education there as he can get anywhere. Furthermore, he will make friends there who will stand by him the rest of his life." He turned upon his son a glance of bitter reproach. "There are very few boys who have had your chance," said he, "and you ought to be grateful instead of turning up your nose at it. Mark my words, you'll live to see the day when you'll thank me for sending you there. Now, I've given you my last word: you'll go where I send you or you'll go nowhere at all."—from LHA*

# THE COLLEGE YEARS
## (1916 - 1920)

IN THE FALL OF 1916 TOM BECAME A FRESHMAN AT THE UNIVERSITY OF NORTH CAROLINA (CALLED PULPIT HILL IN *ANGEL*). IT IS TRUE THAT HE WAS THE VICTIM OF SOME TYPICAL SOPHOMORIC PRANKS THAT YEAR, AND HE DID COME IN FOR HIS SHARE OF GOOD NATURED RIBBING, BUT IT WAS ALL DONE IN A SPIRIT OF FUN. SO, DESPITE THE FACT THAT HE GIVES THE IMPRESSION IN *ANGEL* THAT HE LIVED HIS LIFE AT UNC AS A POOR, MISUNDERSTOOD LONER, AN "UNWASHED GENIUS," HE WAS, ALMOST FROM THE BEGINNING, ONE OF THE MOST POPULAR STUDENTS ON CAMPUS. HE WAS ACTIVE IN EXTRACURRICULAR ACTIVITIES, EDITED THE COLLEGE NEWSPAPER, WROTE PLAYS, SERVED AS AN OFFICER IN VARIOUS CAMPUS ORGANIZATIONS, AND BECAME A MEMBER OF THE PI KAPPA PHI FRATERNITY. HE WAS, IN A WORD, A BIG MAN ON CAMPUS.

TOM AND FRESHMAN ROOMMATE E.A. GRIFFEN (NOTE THAT TOM HAS HIS LEFT HAND RESTING ATOP GRIFFEN'S HEAD).

*Never had a more precious congress of freaks been gathered together under one roof.—from* LHA

IN APRIL OF 1917, DURING TOM'S FRESHMAN YEAR AT UNC, THE UNITED STATES DECLARED WAR AGAINST GERMANY, AND SOON CHAPEL HILL SAW THE EXODUS OF HUNDREDS OF STUDENTS (THOSE TWENTY-ONE YEARS OLD AND OLDER) OFF TO JOIN THE ARMY. THOSE WHO REMAINED WERE HERDED INTO A RIGID MILITARY TRAINING PROGRAM CALLED THE STUDENT ARMY TRAINING CORPS. TOM, OF COURSE, BECAUSE OF HIS AGE, WAS EXEMPT FROM BOTH MILITARY SERVICE AND TRAINING, THOUGH HE VERY ROMANTICALLY VOLUNTEERED HIS SERVICES AND WAS ASSIGNED TO SAT COMPANY C. HERE TOM (BACK ROW, WEARING A WHITE SHIRT) POSES WITH FRIENDS WHO WERE TABBED FOR MILITARY TRAINING.

*In April the nation declared war on Germany. Before the month was out, all the young men at Pulpit Hill who were eligible—those who were twenty-one—were going into service . . . . The fraternity men joined first—those merry and extravagant snobs of whom he had never known, but who now represented for him the highest reach of urbane and aristocratic life.*

*But he wanted to get in. He wanted to be urbane and careless. He wanted to wear well-cut clothes. He wanted to be a gentleman. He wanted to go to war.—from LHA*

IN JUNE OF 1917, DURING HIS SUMMER VACATION, TOM MET A YOUNG LADY WHO WAS SPENDING A FEW WEEKS AT THE OLD KENTUCKY HOME. HER NAME WAS CLARA PAUL (CALLED LAURA JAMES IN *ANGEL*), AND SHE WAS FROM WASHINGTON, N.C. SHE WAS TWENTY-ONE YEARS OLD, SOME FIVE YEARS TOM'S SENIOR, AND ENGAGED TO BE MARRIED. BUT TOM FELL MADLY IN LOVE WITH HER, AND FOR A FEW BEAUTIFUL WEEKS HE THOUGHT SHE WAS IN LOVE WITH HIM. IT WAS HIS FIRST LOVE AFFAIR, ONE THAT HE WOULD REMEMBER WITH SADNESS AND REGRET FOR THE REST OF HIS LIFE.

> *There was at Dixieland a girl named Laura James. She was twenty-one years old. She looked younger. She was there when he came back.*
>
> *Laura was a slender girl, of medium height, but looking taller than she was. She was very firmly moulded: she seemed fresh and washed and clean. She had thick hair, very straight and blonde, combed in a flat bracelet around her small head. Her face was white, with small freckles. Her eyes were soft, candid, cat-green. Her nose was a little too large for her face: it was tilted. She was not pretty. She dressed very simply and elegantly in short plaid skirts and waists of knitted silk.*—from LHA

THIS IS THE CONVERTED PORCH WHERE TOM SLEPT DURING THE SUMMER OF 1917, AND WHERE HE WOULD SLIP CAT-LIKE INTO CLARA'S WINDOW AT NIGHT, RISKING LIFE AND LIMB TO BE WITH HER AFTER EVERYONE ELSE WAS ASLEEP AND THE HOUSE WAS SILENT.

> *They looked, waiting for a spell and the conquest of time. Then she spoke to him—her whisper of his name was only a guess at sound. He threw his leg across the rail, and thrust his long body over space to the sill of her window, stretching out like a cat. She drew her breath in sharply, and cried out softly, No! No! but she caught his arms upon the sills and held him as he twisted in.*
> —from LHA

CLARA PAUL AND FRIENDS. (CLARA HERSELF WROTE THE NAMES ON THIS PHOTO.) IN JULY TOM WAS BROKEN-HEARTED WHEN HE RECEIVED A LETTER FROM CLARA TELLING HIM THAT SHE WOULD NOT RETURN TO ASHEVILLE, THAT SHE WAS IN FACT MARRYING THE MAN TO WHOM SHE HAD BEEN ENGAGED ALL ALONG. SHE WOULD DIE DURING THE FLU EPIDEMIC OF 1918, BUT STILL TOM WOULD NEVER FORGET CLARA. SOME TEN YEARS LATER, WHEN WRITING *ANGEL,* HE WOULD COMPOSE THE FOLLOWING HAUNTINGLY POIGNANT LINES:

*Come up into the hills, O my young love. Return! O lost, and by the wind grieved, ghost, come back again, as first I knew you in the timeless valley, where we shall feel ourselves anew, bedded on magic in the month of June. There was a place where all the sun went glistening in your hair, and from the hill we could have put a finger on a star. Where is the day that melted into one rich noise? Where the music of your flesh, the rhyme of your teeth, the dainty languor of your legs, your small firm arms, your slender fingers, to be bitten like an apple, and the little cherry-teats of your white breasts? And where are all the fine wires of finespun maidenhair? Quick are the months of earth, and quick the teeth that fed upon this loveliness. You who were made for music, will hear music no more: in your dark house the winds are silent. Ghost, ghost, come back from that marriage that we did not foresee, return not into life, but into magic, where we have never died, into the enchanted wood, where we still lie, strewn on the grass. Come up into the hills, O my young love: return. O lost, and by the wind grieved, ghost, come back again.—from* LHA

Tom was devastated to learn of Clara's marriage, and for months afterward his emotions alternated between pain and anger. His immediate reaction was to lash out at his family, and in a moment of insane fury he rushed to the rear of the Old Kentucky Home where, like Samson, he would pull down the temple that had spawned the great hurt of his life.

*The yard sloped sharply down: the gaunt back of Dixieland was propped upon a dozen rotting columns of whitewashed brick, fourteen feet high. In the dim light, by one of these slender piers, already mined with crumbling ruins of wet brick, the scarecrow crouched, toiling with the thin grapevine of his arms against the temple.*

*"I will kill you, House," he gasped. "Vile and accursed House, I will tear you down. I will bring you down upon the whores and boarders. I will wreck you, House."—from LHA*

In August of 1917, Fred, in a frenzy of patriotic fervor, joined the navy, and, after a brief training period, found himself stationed in Norfolk, Virginia. Typically, he would soon inform everyone that he was "fighting to make the world safe for hypocricy."

*Luke had given up his employment in a war-munitions factory at Dayton, Ohio, and had enlisted in the Navy. He had come home on a short leave before his departure for the training-school at Newport, Rhode Island. The street roared as he came down at his vulgar wide-legged stride, in flapping blues, his face all on the grin, thick curls of his unruly hair coiling below the band of his hat. He was the cartoon of a gob.—from LHA*

TOM AS A SOPHOMORE AT UNC IN THE FALL OF 1917.

*In this strange place Eugene flourished amazingly. He was outside the pale of popular jealousies: it was quite obvious that he was not safe, that he was not sound, that decidedly he was an irregular person. He could never be an all-around man. Obviously, he would never be governor. Obviously, he would never be a politician, because he said funny things. He was not the man to lead a class or say a prayer; he was a man for curious enterprise. Well, thought they benevolently, we need some such. We are not all made for weighty business.*
—*from* LHA

TOM IN 1917 AT AN UNKNOWN LOCATION WITH UNKNOWN PEOPLE. BASED ON THIS PHOTO IT SEEMS SAFE TO CONCLUDE THAT TOM WAS, IN REALITY, HARDLY THE SCORNED MISANTHOROPE THAT WE MEET IN EUGENE GANT OF *LOOK HOMEWARD, ANGEL*. IN FACT, HE WAS A VERY HANDSOME AND QUITE SOCIABLE YOUNG MAN.

AMONG HIS MANY OTHER ACHIEVEMENTS OF 1917–18, TOM WAS ELECTED TO THE UNC DIALECTIC SOCIETY.

TOM WENT HOME FOR THE CHRISTMAS HOLIDAYS IN 1917 AND WAS SHOCKED AT HIS FATHER'S WASTED APPEARANCE. W.O. HAD BEEN DIAGNOSED AT JOHNS HOPKINS AS SUFFERING FROM CANCER OF THE PROSTATE . HE WOULD DIE OF THIS ILLNESS IN 1922.

*Abruptly, Eugene was touched with pity. For the first time he saw plainly that great Gant had grown old. The sallow face had yellowed and lost its sinew. The thin mouth was petulant. The chemistry of decay had left its mark.*

*No, there was no return after this. Eugene saw now that Gant was dying very slowly. The vast resiliency, the illimitable power of former times had vanished. The big frame was breaking up before him like a beached ship. Gant was sick. He was old.*

*Gant had aged and wasted shockingly. His heavy clothes wound round his feeble shanks: his face was waxen and transparent--it was like a great beak. He looked clean and fragile. The cancer, Eugene thought, flowered in him like some terrible but beautiful plant. His mind was very clear, not doting, but sad and old. He spoke little, with almost comical gentleness, but he ceased to listen almost as soon as one answered.*
*—from LHA*

IN THE SUMMER OF 1918, FOLLOWING HIS VERY SUCCESSFUL SOPHOMORE YEAR AT UNC, TOM WOULD VISIT ASHEVILLE BRIEFLY BEFORE LEAVING FOR NORFOLK, VIRGINIA, WHERE HE HOPED TO FIND WORK IN A WARTIME INSTALLATION. IT WAS TIME TO DECLARE HIS INDEPENDENCE FROM HIS PARENTS, SAID TOM. BUT IN TRUTH HE KNEW THAT CLARA PAUL AND HER NEW HUSBAND WERE LIVING IN NEARBY PORTSMOUTH, AND HE PRAYED TO CATCH A GLIMPSE OF HER, PERHAPS EVEN TO MEET HER ON THE STREET.

BEN GAVE HIM MONEY AND IMPLORED JULIA AND W.O. TO LET TOM GO. FRED (IN THE PHOTO ABOVE) WAS STATIONED IN NORFOLK AND WOULD CERTAINLY LOOK AFTER TOM SHOULD HE NEED HELP. W.O. AND JULIA, AFTER MUCH HESITATION, RELUCTANTLY AGREED.

SUBSEQUENTLY, TOM, STILL ONLY SEVENTEEN, SPENT A ROUGH AND TUMBLE SUMMER LOADING AND UNLOADING SHIPS, DIGGING DITCHES, AND MAKING GREAT EFFORTS NOT TO STARVE TO DEATH. HE DID FIND THE HOUSE WHERE CLARA WAS LIVING, BUT MADE NO ATTEMPT TO CONTACT HER. AT THIS TIME SHE HAD ONLY MONTHS TO LIVE.

IT WAS DURING HIS JUNIOR YEAR AT UNC THAT TOM TRULY HIT HIS STRIDE AS A BIG MAN ON CAMPUS. HERE (STANDING IN CENTER) HE WAS INDUCTED INTO THE GOLDEN FLEECE, THE OLDEST HONOR SOCIETY ON CAMPUS. IN THE PHOTO BELOW TOM (CENTER) RELAXES ON THE PORCH OF THE PI KAPPA PHI FRATERNITY HOUSE.

*He began to join. He joined everything. He had never "belonged" to any group before, but now all groups were beckoning him. He had without much trouble won a place for himself on the staff of the college paper and the magazine. The small beginning trickle of distinctions widened into a gushet. It began to sprinkle, then it rained. He was initiated into literary fraternities, dramatic fraternities, theatrical fraternities, speaking fraternities, journalistic fraternities, and in the Spring into a social fraternity. He joined enthusiastically, submitted with fanatical glee to the hard mauling of the initiations, and went about lame and sore, more pleased than a child or a savage, with colored ribbons in his coat lapel, and a waistcoat plastered with pins, badges, symbols, and Greek lettering.—from LHA*

In September of 1918 Tom paid a weekend visit home to enjoy a family reunion at 92 Woodfin. Within weeks of this happy occasion Ben would be dead of pneumonia. (L-R:) Tom, Julia, W.O., Frank, Dietz, Margaret, Effie and four of her children, Fred, Mabel, and Ben.

The handsome, soft-spoken Ben, ever a favorite with the ladies, had been working in the ad department of a Winston-Salem newspaper when he visited Asheville for the reunion.

DETAILS OF THE REUNION PHOTOGRAPH ON THE PREVIOUS PAGE.

EFFIE'S CHILDREN, LEFT FOR A VISIT WITH THEIR GRANDPARENTS IN ASHEVILLE, HAD BEEN SUFFERING FROM THE FLU. IT IS SUGGESTED THAT BEN BECAME ILL AS A RESULT OF A VIRUS CAUGHT FROM ONE OF THESE CHILDREN. A FEW WEEKS AFTER ARRIVING BACK AT COLLEGE, TOM RECEIVED WORD OF BEN'S ILLNESS FROM HIS FATHER.

> *"Daisy has been here with all her tribe. She went home two days ago, leaving Caroline and Richard. They have been down sick with the flu. We've had a siege of it here. Every one has had it, and you never know who's going to be next."*
>
> *He heard nothing more for several weeks. Then, one drizzling evening at six o'clock, when he returned to the room that he occupied with Heston, he found a telegram. It read: "Come home at once. Ben has pneumonia. Mother."*—from **LHA**

IT WAS EARLY EVENING IN OCTOBER, JUST A WEEK AFTER TOM'S BIRTHDAY, WHEN HE ARRIVED HOME TO FIND BEN ON HIS DEATHBED. TOM WAS DEVASTATED.

> *"Ben's in that room upstairs," Luke whispered, "where the light is."*
>
> *Eugene looked up with cold dry lips to the bleak front room upstairs, with its ugly Victorian bay-window. It was next to the sleeping-porch where, but three weeks before, Ben had hurled into the darkness his savage curse at life. The light in the sickroom burned grayly, bringing to him its grim vision of struggle and naked terror.*—from **LHA**

THIS IS THE BED IN THE DRAB UPSTAIRS BEDROOM, NOW CAREFULLY PRESERVED AT THE OLD KENTUCKY HOME, WHERE BEN, TOM'S IDOL, DIED IN 1918.

*The only sound in the room now was the low rattling mutter of Ben's breath. He no longer gasped; he no longer gave signs of consciousness or struggle. His eyes were almost closed; their gray flicker was dulled, coated with the sheen of insensibility and death. He lay quietly upon his back, very straight, without sign of pain, and with a curious upturned thrust of his sharp thin face. His mouth was firmly shut. Already, save for the feeble mutter of his breath, he seemed to be dead—he seemed detached, no part of the ugly mechanism of that sound which came to remind them of the terrible chemistry of flesh, to mock at illusion, at all belief in the strange passage and continuance of life.—from* LHA

BEN WOLFE ABOUT 1915.

*We can believe in the nothingness of life, we can believe in the nothingness of death and of life after death—but who can believe in the nothingness of Ben? Like Apollo, who did his penance to the high god in the sad house of King Admetus, he came, a god with broken feet, into the gray hovel of this world. And he lived here a stranger, trying to recapture the music of the lost world, trying to recall the great forgotten language, the lost faces, the stone, the leaf, the door.*

*O Artemidorus, farewell!—from* LHA

BY THE SPRING OF 1919, TOM'S JUNIOR YEAR, HE HAD ESTABLISHED HIMSELF AS NOT ONLY ONE OF THE LEADING SCHOLARS ON CAMPUS BUT ALSO AS THE FINEST WRITER IN THE HISTORY OF THE COLLEGE. ACCORDING TO A POPULAR STORY, THE ATHLETIC DEPARTMENT AT UNC CLAIMED THAT THE FOOTBALL TEAM WOULD DO BETTER IF THEY HAD THE SUPPORT OF THE COLLEGE NEWSPAPER. THUS TOM, AS EDITOR OF *THE DAILY TAR HEEL*, VISITED WITH THE COACH AND PROMISED THAT HE WOULD WRITE NO MORE EDITORIALS CRITICAL OF THE TEAM. THE FOLLOWING SATURDAY UNC FELL TO A WEAK VMI TEAM, AND TOM, IN A DISPLAY OF HIS SHARP SENSE OF HUMOR, WROTE THE FOLLOWING TONGUE-IN-CHEEK ACCOUNT OF THE GAME: "ON THE FIRST PLAY FROM SCRIMMAGE, A KEYDET HALFBACK SKIRTED RIGHT END FOR SIXTY YARDS, ONLY TO BE STOPPED DEAD IN HIS TRACKS BY AN ALERT CAROLINA DEFENSE."

IN THE ABOVE PHOTO TOM IS PICTURED ALONG WITH SEVERAL OTHER CAMPUS "LITERARY GIANTS" IN 1919. THE GENTLEMAN SEATED TO THE FAR RIGHT IS JOHN TERRY OF ROCKINGHAM, N.C., WHO, FOLLOWING TOM'S DEATH IN 1938, WAS APPOINTED HIS OFFICIAL BIOGRAPHER. THOUGH HE GATHERED A GREAT DEAL OF MATERIAL, TERRY HAD WRITTEN NOTHING ON WOLFE AT THE TIME OF HIS OWN DEATH IN 1953. NOTE THAT TERRY, IN THE PHOTO ABOVE, IS HOLDING A LITTLE VOLUME ENTITLED *POETS OF THE FUTURE*.

## The Carolina Playmakers
### The University of North Carolina

ANNOUNCE THEIR OPENING PERFORMANCE
IN
### THE PLAY-HOUSE
CHAPEL HILL
A PROGRAM CONSISTING OF THE

# Original Folk Plays

**WHEN WITCHES RIDE**
A Play of Carolina Folk Superstition, by Elizabeth Lay

**THE RETURN OF BUCK GAVIN**
A Tragedy of the Mountain People, by Thomas Wolfe

**Together With**

**WHAT WILL BARBARA SAY!**
A Romance of Chapel Hill, by Minnie Shepherd Sparrow

**Friday and Saturday, March 14th and 15th, 1919**
All Seats Reserved at Eubanks' Drug Store, Chapel Hill
**Curtain Promptly at Eight O'clock**

IN MARCH OF 1919 THE CAROLINA PLAYMAKERS STAGED TOM'S *THE RETURN OF BUCK GAVIN*, A STORY SET IN THE NORTH CAROLINA MOUNTAINS. THIS DRAMA WOULD BE PRESENTED FOR MANY YEARS TO COME.

Not only did Tom write the play, but then, when a suitable leading man could not be found, he himself very modestly volunteered to play Buck Gavin. Those who witnessed the play say that he turned in a creditable performance. Of course, he was no newcomer to the stage, having been an eager participant in school productions and declamation contests as a boy in Asheville. In fact, neither Tom nor any of his siblings was ever shy when it came to performing in public, certainly a testimonial to their parents and teachers.

ANOTHER OF TOM'S PLAYS, *THE THIRD NIGHT*, WAS STAGED ON DECEMBER 12, 1919.
(L-R:) JONATHAN DANIELS, FREDERICK COHN, AND TOM.

### THOMAS CLAYTON WOLFE
#### ASHEVILLE, N. C.
*Age, 19; Weight, 178; Height, 6 feet 3 inches*

Di Society; Buncombe County Club; Freshman-Sophomore
Debate (2); Dramatic Association; Carolina Playmakers (3, 4),
Author two One-Act Plays, Executive Committee (4); Associate
Editor YACKETY YACK (3); Associate Editor *Magazine* (3);
Assistant Editor-in-Chief (4); Managing Editor *Tar Heel* (3);
Editor-in-Chief (4); Advisory Board *Tar Baby* (4); Worth Prize
in Philosophy (3); Y. M. C. A. Cabinet (3, 4); Student Council
(4); Athletic Council (4); Class Poet (3, 4); Chairman Junior
Stunt Committee; German Club; Amphoterothen; Satyrs;
Golden Fleece.

Σ Υ; Ω Δ; Π Κ Φ.

EDITING the *Tar Heel*, winning Horace's
philosophy prize when only a Junior, writing
plays and then showing the world how they
should be acted—they are all alike to this young
Shakespeare. Last year he played the leading
role in the "Midnight Frolic" at "Gooch's Winter
Palace", but this year it's the leading role on
the "Carolina Shipping Board". But, seriously
speaking, "Buck" is a great, big fellow. He can
do more between 8:25 and 8:30 than the rest of
us can do all day, and it is no wonder that he is
classed as a genius.

A PAGE FROM THE 1920 UNC YEARBOOK ATTESTING TO TOM'S SUCCESS AS
A STUDENT. THE SKETCH AT THE BOTTOM OF THIS PAGE IS A GOOD-NATURED
CARICATURE OF TOM IN HIS ROLE AS BUCK GAVIN.

TOM'S GRADUATING CLASS. HE IS STANDING IN THE BACK ROW, JUST ABOVE THE "2" ON THE 1920 PENNANT. HIS GREAT PLAN NOW, SHOULD HE BE ABLE TO PERSUADE HIS PARENTS TO SEND HIM, WAS TO ENROLL IN PROFESSOR GEORGE PIERCE BAKER'S PLAY-WRITING CLASS (THE 47 WORKSHOP) AT HARVARD UNIVERSITY. TOM GRADUATED FROM HARVARD IN 1922, AND PUBLISHED *LOOK HOMEWARD, ANGEL* IN 1929. THE REST IS HISTORY.

---

*Gant and Eliza came to his graduation. He found them lodging in the town: it was early June—hot, green, fiercely and voluptuously Southern. The campus was a green oven; the old grads went about in greasy pairs; the cool pretty girls, who never sweated, came in to see their young men graduate, and to dance; the mamas and papas were shown about dumbly and shyly.*

*The college was charming, half-deserted. Most of the students, except the graduating class, had departed. The air was charged with the fresh sensual heat, the deep green shimmer of heavy leafage, a thousand spermy earth and flower-scents. The young men were touched with sadness, with groping excitement, with glory.—from LHA*

A Charles Scribner's publicity shot taken of Tom in 1929, immediately following the publication of *Look Homeward, Angel*.

# A Chronology of Events in the Life of Thomas Wolfe

| | | |
|---|---|---|
| 1885 | Jan | W.O. Wolfe and Julia Westall are married. |
| 1886 | | Baby Leslie is born. Leslie will die of infant cholera at the age of 10 months. |
| 1887 | | Effie is born. |
| 1888 | | Frank is born. |
| 1890 | | Mabel is born. |
| 1892 | | The twins, Ben and Grover, are born. |
| 1894 | | Fred is born. |
| 1900 | Oct | Thomas Clayton Wolfe is born. |
| 1904 | Nov | Grover dies in St. Louis during the World's Fair. |
| 1905 | Sept | Tom enters the Orange Street public school. |
| 1906 | Aug | Julia buys the Old Kentucky Home. |
| 1912 | Sept | Tom enters the North State Fitting School and meets Margaret Roberts. |
| 1916 | Sept | Tom graduates from North State and enters the University of North Carolina. |
| 1917 | Apr | The United States enters World War I. |
| | June | Tom has his relationship with Clara Paul. |
| 1918 | June | Tom spends the summer in Norfolk, Virginia. |
| | Oct | Ben dies. |
| | Nov | World War I ends. |
| 1919 | Mar | The Carolina Playmakers stage *The Return of Buck Gavin*. |
| 1920 | May | Tom graduates from the University of North Carolina. |
| | Sept | Tom enters Harvard University and enrolls in George Pierce Baker's 47 Workshop. He also meets Kenneth Raisbeck. |

| 1921 | Oct | The 47 Workshop stages *The Mountains*. |
| 1922 | June | W.O. dies of cancer. |
| 1923 | May | The 47 Workshop stages *Welcome to Our City*. |
| 1924 | Feb | After receiving his master's degree from Harvard, Tom begins teaching at NYU. |
| | Oct | Tom takes his first trip to Europe. |
| 1925 | Aug | Tom meets Aline Bernstein aboard the *Olympic*. |
| | Sept | Tom resumes teaching duties at NYU. |
| 1926 | June | Tom goes abroad with Aline. |
| | July | Tom begins first draft of *Look Homeward, Angel* (originally titled, *O, Lost*). |
| | Aug | Aline returns to America, while Tom remains in England to work on his novel. |
| | Dec | Tom first visits Germany, the homeland of his ancestors. |
| 1927 | Jan | Tom returns to New York City and continues work on his novel while living in an Eighth Street loft. |
| | July | Tom again goes abroad with Aline. |
| | Sept | Tom resumes teaching duties at NYU. |
| 1928 | Mar | Tom completes manuscript of *Look Homeward, Angel*. |
| | June | Tom again goes abroad, leaving manuscript with his agent. |
| | Nov | Tom receives a letter from Maxwell Perkins expressing interest in publishing *Angel*. |
| 1929 | Jan | Tom meets Perkins, then resumes teaching at NYU while revising his novel. |
| | Aug | "The Angel on the Porch" is published by *Scribners Magazine*. |
| | Oct | *Look Homeward, Angel* is published. (The stock market crashes one week later.) |
| 1930 | May | Having resigned from NYU and having received a Guggenheim Fellowship, Tom again travels to Europe. |
| | June | Tom meets F. Scott Fitzgerald in Paris. |
| | Oct | Tom settles in London. |
| 1931 | Feb | Tom meets Sinclair Lewis. |
| | Mar | Tom returns to New York and settles in Brooklyn. Aline Bernstein attempts suicide. |
| 1932 | Apr | "A Portrait of Bascome Hawke" is published in *Scribners Magazine*. (In July this story will tie for first place in Scribners $5,000 best short novel contest.) |
| 1933 | Jan | Maxwell Perkins persuades Tom to resume the story of Eugene Gant where he stopped it in *Angel*. The result will be *Of Time and the River*. |

| 1934 | Sept | Despite Tom's protests, Perkins sends the manuscript of *Of Time and the River* to the printer. |
| 1935 | Mar | Tom goes abroad. Perkins wires him that *Of Time and the River* has been published. |
| | May | Tom visits Berlin to find that his novels and name are famous in Germany. |
| | July | Tom returns to America and attends the University of Colorado Writer's Conference. |
| | Sept | Tom settles at 865 First Avenue, New York City. |
| | Nov | *From Death to Morning* is published. |
| 1936 | Apr | *The Story of a Novel* is published. It is attacked by Bernard De Voto in an article entitled "Genius is Not Enough." |
| | Aug | Tom again visits Germany, this time during the Olympics. |
| 1937 | Mar | "I Have a Thing to Tell You" serialized in *The New Republic*. |
| | May | Tom visits Asheville for the first time since the publication of *Angel*. |
| | July | Tom rents the cabin at Oteen. |
| | Dec | Tom breaks with Scribners and signs a contract with Harpers. |
| 1938 | May | Tom completes the "George Webber" manuscript. |
| | June | Tom tours the national parks. |
| | July | Tom is taken ill with pneumonia and hospitalized at Firlawn Sanitarium near Seattle, Washington. |
| | Aug | Tom is transferred to Providence Hospital in Seattle. |
| | Sept | Tom is transferred to Baltimore and operated on at Johns Hopkins Hospital, but dies a few days later, at 5:30 a.m., September 15, just eighteen days short of his thirty-eighth birthday. |

# SELECTED BIBLIOGRAPHY

**Note: In addition to the selections listed below, students of Thomas Wolfe might wish to consult** *The Thomas Wolfe Review*, **a publication of the Thomas Wolfe Society.**

Adams, Agatha Boyd. *Thomas Wolfe, Carolina Student* (Chapel Hill: UNC Library, 1950).

Daniels, Jonathan. *Thomas Wolfe: October Recollections* (Columbia, S.C.: Bostick & Thornley, 1961).

Donald, David H. *Look Homeward: A Life of Thomas Wolfe* (Boston: Little, Brown & Co., 1987).

Field, Leslie A. *Thomas Wolfe: Three Decades of Criticism* (New York: NYU Press, 1968).

Holman, C. Hugh *Thomas Wolfe* (Minneapolis: University of Minnesota Press, 1960).

————*The World of Thomas Wolfe* (New York: Charles Scribner's, 1962).

————*The Loneliness at the Core* (Baton Rouge: LSU Press, 1975).

Idol, John L. *A Thomas Wolfe Companion* (New York: Greenwood Press, 1987).

Johnson, Pamela H. *The Art of Thomas Wolfe* (New York: Charles Scribners, 1963).

Johnston, Carol. *Thomas Wolfe: A Descriptive Bibliography* (Pittsburgh: University of Pittsburgh Press, 1987).

Kennedy, Richard S. *The Window of Memory: The Literary Career of Thomas Wolfe* (Chapel Hill: UNC Press, 1962).

Klein, Carole. *Aline* (New York: Harper & Row, 1979).

McElderry, Bruce R. *Thomas Wolfe* (New York: Twayne Publishers, 1964).

Nowell, Elizabeth. *Thomas Wolfe: A Biography* (Westport, Conn.: Greenwood Press, 1972).

Phillipson, John S. *Critical Essays on Thomas Wolfe* (Boston: G. K. Hall, 1985).

Pollock, Thomas C. *Thomas Wolfe at Washington Square* (New York: NYU Press, 1954).

Reeves, Paschal. *The Merrill Studies in "Look Homeward, Angel"* (Columbus, Ohio: C. E. Merrill, 1970).

Rubin, Louis D. *Thomas Wolfe: The Weather of His Youth* (Baton Rouge: LSU Press, 1955).

———*Thomas Wolfe: A Collection of Critical Essays* (Englewood Cliffs, N.J.: Prentice-Hall, 1973).

Teicher, Morton I. *Looking Homeward: A Thomas Wolfe Photo Album* (Columbia, Mo.: University of Missouri Press, 1993).

Turnbull, Andrew. *Thomas Wolfe* (New York: Charles Scribner's, 1968).

Walser, Richard G. *The Enigma of Thomas Wolfe: Biographical and Critical Selections* (Cambridge: Harvard University Press, 1953).

———*Thomas Wolfe: An Introduction and Interpretation* (New York: Barnes & Noble, 1961).

———*Thomas Wolfe, Undergraduate* (Durham: Duke University Press, 1977).

Watkins, Floyd C. *Thomas Wolfe's Characters: Portraits of Life* (Norman: University of Oklahoma Press, 1957).

Wheaton, Mabel (Wolfe). *Thomas Wolfe and His Family* (Garden City, N.Y.: Doubleday, 1961).

Wisdom, William B. *The Table Talk of Thomas Wolfe.* (An Aldo P. Magi Book: The Thomas Wolfe Society, 1988).

Wolfe, Thomas C. *Look Homeward, Angel* (New York: Charles Scribner's, 1929).

———*Of Time and The River* (New York: Charles Scribner's, 1935).

———*From Death to Morning* (New York: Charles Scribner's, 1935).

———*The Story of a Novel* (New York: Charles Scribner's, 1936).

———*The Web and the Rock* (New York: Harper, 1939).

———*The Face of a Nation* (New York: Charles Scribner's, 1939).

Wolfe, Thomas C. *(continued)*

————*You Can't Go Home Again* (New York: Harper, 1940).

————*The Hills Beyond* (New York: Harper, 1941).

————*A Stone, A Leaf, A Door* (New York: Charles Scribner's, 1945).

————*Mannerhouse* (New York: Harper, 1948).

————*A Western Journal* (Pittsburgh: University of Pittsburgh Press, 1951).

————*The Short Novels of Thomas Wolfe*, ed C. Hugh Holman (New York: Charles Scribner's, 1961).

————*The Mountains*, ed. Pat M. Ryan (Chapel Hill: UNC Press, 1970).

————*The Notebooks of Thomas Wolfe*, 2 volumes, ed. Richard S. Kennedy and Paschal Reeves (Chapel Hill: UNC Press, 1970).

————*The Autobiography of an American Novelist.* (Cambridge: Harvard University Press, 1983).

————*The Autobiographical Outline for "Look Homeward, Angel."* ( The Thomas Wolfe Society, 1991).

————*The Lost Boy* (Chapel Hill: UNC Press, 1992).